Robert H. Albers, PhD

Shame: A Faith Perspective

Pre-publication
REVIEWS,
COMMENTARIES,
EVALUATIONS . . .

"**D**r. Albers' book describes a 'shame-based' identity–those people who feel they have little worth or value. He argues that inherent within the Judeo-Christian tradition is a world of liberation not only for those who are oppressed by guilt, but also for those who are bound up in shame.

Shame goes beyond present-day writings on the psychology of shame by relating these understandings of shame to the faith tradition. It is not just another book that describes shame but one that points to transformation that comes from God.

The chapter on theological resources from the faith tradition is especially insightful. It is 'must' reading for ministers who offer care for shame-based individuals."

Howard W. Stone
Professor, Pastoral Theology
and Pastoral Counseling,
Brite Divinity School,
Texas Christian University

More pre-publication
REVIEWS, COMMENTARIES, EVALUATIONS . . .

"**I** n this lucid and well-written book, pastors will find an excellent pastoral theological discussion of the pervasive and long-neglected problem of shame. Dr. Albers focuses on 'disgrace shame,' a deep sense of unworthiness that pervades and undermines the personality and interpersonal relations of many people in our time. Drawing on recent research and theory, he skillfully describes its many forms and dynamics, showing how shame is woven into the texture of everyday life and how it often underlies guilt, complicating the quest for forgiveness and peace.

Albers sets his whole discussion in a theological perspective and offers insightful, practical guidelines for pastoral response. *Shame: A Faith Perspective* makes a significant and useful contribution to pastoral theological literature. It deserves a wide and careful reading among parish ministers, priests, rabbis, and pastoral counselors. It could also be read with profit by secular counselors and psychotherapists."

Rodney J. Hunter, PhD
Professor of Pastoral Theology,
Candler School of Theology,
Emory University

"**T**he theological proposal of this book goes far beyond being just another call for the translation of biblical directives into culturally relevant terms. Dr. Albers distinguishes clearly between guilt and shame, then opens up the meaning and dynamics of the shame we all know, even across cultures, but do not all know how to address either in ourselves or as we seek to help each other. He then urges us, honestly moved by his own experience of shame, to receive anew the healing power available in and through the deep symbols we may yet creatively share in Christian community. 'Creatively' means for Albers what will appear surprising or even contradicting to some, that the Spirit's gracious gifts and fruits may be shared in simple ritual ways to transform lives.

Shame: A Faith Perspective is about helping one another through the threat of death, at whatever level that might occur, and back to life. Albers offers us new, yet familiar, resources for a creative participation in tht gracious process."

Thomas C. Christensen, ThD
Co-Pastor, Harbour Pointe
Evangelical Lutheran Church;
Professor, Meiganga Seminary;
Author of *An African Tree of Life*

More pre-publication
REVIEWS, COMMENTARIES, EVALUATIONS . . .

"**R**obert Albers engages readers with the reality of shame and the pressing need for Christian communities to address this reality. Albers assumes that 'shame based identity' is grounded in a sense of worthlessness and that the Christian faith tradition offers 'a powerful world of liberation.'

Drawing upon biblical interpretation, psychological theories, and case material, Albers distinguishes between shame and guilt. As he describes the dynamics of 'disgrace shame,' he casts a bright light on such common human experiences as desertion, dishonor, defectiveness, and defilement. Further, Albers challenges and expands traditional Christian doctrines; he enlarges the meaning of justification to include an affirmation of human worth, and he reinterprets Jesus as one who carried the shame of the world in His life and death.

Albers proposes ways to dismantle shame by encouraging spiritual practices in community life, counseling relationships, and daily living. Expanding upon contemporary psychology, he offers a guide that is replete with examples from his experience and clear suggestions for action."

Mary Elizabeth Moore, PhD
Professor of Theology
and Christian Education,
School of Theology at Claremont

The Haworth Pastoral Press
An Imprint of The Haworth Press, Inc.

NOTES FOR PROFESSIONAL LIBRARIANS
AND LIBRARY USERS

This is an original book title published by The Haworth Pastoral Press, an imprint of The Haworth Press, Inc. Unless otherwise noted in specific chapters with attribution, materials in this book have not been previously published elsewhere in any format or language.

CONSERVATION AND PRESERVATION NOTES

All books published by The Haworth Press, Inc. and its imprints are printed on certified ph neutral, acid free book grade paper. This paper meets the minimum requirements of American National Standard for Information Sciences–Permanence of Paper for Printed Material, ANSI Z39.48-1984.

Shame
A Faith Perspective

Colorado Christian University
Library
180 S. Garrison
Lakewood, Colorado 80226

The Haworth Pastoral Press
Religion, Ministry & Pastoral Care
William M. Clements, PhD
Senior Editor

New, Recent, and Forthcoming Titles:

Growing Up: Pastoral Nurture for the Later Years by Thomas B. Robb

Religion and Family: When God Helps by Laurel Arthur Burton

Victims of Dementia: Services, Support, and Care by Wm. Michael Clemmer

Horrific Traumata: A Pastoral Response to the Post-Traumatic Stress Disorder by N. Duncan Sinclair

Aging and God: Spiritual Pathways to Mental Health in Midlife and Later Years by Harold G. Koenig

Counseling for Spiritually Empowered Wholeness: A Hope-Centered Approach by Howard Clinebell

Shame: A Faith Perspective by Robert H. Albers

Shame
A Faith Perspective

Robert H. Albers, PhD

The Haworth Pastoral Press
An Imprint of The Haworth Press, Inc.
New York • London

© 1995 by The Haworth Press, Inc. All rights reserved. No part of this work may be reproduced or utilized in any form or by any means, electronic or mechanical, including photocopying, microfilm and recording, or by any information storage and retrieval system, without permission in writing from the publisher. Printed in the United States of America.

The Haworth Pastoral Press, an imprint of The Haworth Press, Inc., 10 Alice Street, Binghamton, NY 13904-1580

Library of Congress Cataloging-in-Publication Data

Albers, Robert H.
    Shame : a faith perspective / Robert H. Albers.
        p. cm.
    Includes bibliographical references (p.   ) and index.
    ISBN 1-56024-935-8 (alk. paper)
    1. Shame–Religious aspects–Christianity. I. Title.
BT714.A43 1995
233–dc20   94-29610
                                                                                  CIP

This book is dedicated
to my whole family
and
in loving memory
of my dad

ABOUT THE AUTHOR

Robert H. Albers, PhD, MDiv, is Professor of Pastoral Theology and Ministry at Luther Seminary in St. Paul, Minnesota. His interest in the topic of shame grew out of his extensive pastoral and professional work dealing with individuals afflicted and affected by chemical dependency. He has conducted scores of seminars throughout the United States with pastors and other professionals on the topic of shame. Dr. Albers served for 14 years as a Lutheran pastor in Corby, England and Blair, Nebraska, and served several interim pastorates in southern California while completing his doctoral work. He is Editor of the *Journal of Ministry in Addiction & Recovery.*

CONTENTS

Foreword

Robert Albers presents an insightful, highly readable understanding of disgrace shame that integrates the faith tradition with psychological theory. While there are many resources that discuss shame from a psychological perspective, this book explores how God's gifts of love, acceptance, and forgiveness can heal our shame-based identity and empower us to accept our God-given identity as loved people.

This book is grounded in scholarly research, as well as in practical hands-on ideas for how to dismantle the shame that binds and immobilizes people. Robert Albers offers the reader compassionate and thoughtful reflections on how faith in Christ enables people to move beyond a shame-based identity and boldly accept and celebrate a grace-filled identity. This book contains helpful suggestions and resources for people to heal spiritually, emotionally, intellectually, and relationally.

Disgrace shame is a tragic reality in many people's lives. This book offers powerful resources for healing and developing a sense of identity rooted in God's love and forgiveness. I highly recommend this book to clergy, counselors, and others in the healing professions, as well as to all those experiencing the desolation of shame.

Rev. Anne Marie Nuechterlein, PhD
Wartburg Theological Seminary

Acknowledgements

The completion of a task is never accomplished without the assistance, forbearance, and cooperation of many people. The writing of this book is no exception, as there are several personal and professional acknowledgements that need to be made.

Beginning with the personal acknowledgements, I wish to express gratitude to my whole family, but particularly to my wife Sonia and our three children Joyce, Stephen, and Joel, who put up with the mass of books and the mess of paper that often accumulated around the family computer. Their tolerance and patience with this rather involved process merits my special gratitude. The encouragement and support from all of them, as well as that received from our new daughter-in-law, Heidi, in the final stages of this work was most appreciated.

A special word of thanks is extended to Dr. William Clements, Professor of pastoral care and counseling at the Southern California School of Theology in Claremont. Bill is also the senior religion editor at The Haworth Press and his enthusiasm and encouragement were the key factors in my returning to the manuscript, revising it, and completing it for publication. Without his professional and personal support for this project, this book would not have seen the light of day!

To my friends and colleagues, Carol Baker, Terence Fretheim, Mary Knutson, and Bill Smith, who provided substantive as well as editorial critiques as the manuscript was being developed, my deep gratitude. A special word of thanks to my colleague Anne Marie Nuechterlein who teaches at my beloved alma mater, Wartburg Theological Seminary. She not only provided excellent feedback, but also was gracious enough to write the foreword. Words are inadequate to express my thanks to her.

Several people read through the manuscript and provided important suggestions. Among them are: Libby Jensen, Nancy Lindblad,

Janet Wheelock, and several students, many of whom I can no longer name. At the risk of omitting one of their names, I simply acknowledge the important contributions they made to the conversation concerning this subject.

Often unacknowledged are the wonderful people behind the scenes who do the difficult work of typing. To Ms. Ruth Klett, who did much of the early typing; to Ms. Janet Lindell Thorson, who patiently and graciously did all of the technical work of transmitting the manuscript from one computer system to another and who accomplished the laborious task of correction and revision; and finally, to Ms. Dianne Jelle and Ms. Deb Noel, who completed the final entries involving changes and revisions, my deep gratitude and appreciation. A special word of thanks is extended to Ms. Sharon Firle, my teaching assistant, for completing the laborious task of indexing the book. I would also like to acknowledge and thank Elizabeth Harman for creating the design for the cover.

Finally, on the personal level, to the many people in various congregations as well as pastors who continually asked when this book would be finished, my thanks for your gentle pressure to bring this project to completion. Even though the names, circumstances, and details have been changed to protect the identity of my counselees, I owe all of them a debt of thanks as they have taught me about the power and pervasiveness of disgrace shame from their life experiences and aided in raising my own consciousness about my personal shame issues.

On the professional level, my gratitude is expressed to the board, administration, and faculty of Luther Northwestern Theological Seminary for making it possible for me to have a sabbatical year in which most of the research and much of the writing was accomplished. The substantial monetary grant provided by the Lutheran Brotherhood Insurance Company was deeply appreciated and eased the financial situation during my sabbatical year.

A special word of commendation to the administration and faculty of the Southern California School of Theology in Claremont. Dean Allen Moore's invitation to be a scholar-in-residence, coupled with the hospitality accorded me for the semester I was in Claremont with all of the privileges granted for library work, research, and office space, was deeply appreciated. It was a pleasure to return to the School of Theology, seven years after having completed my graduate program there, to renew acquaintances in the area and to establish new friendships.

There is always the danger in delineating acknowledgements that someone who was crucial in the completion of the task might be omitted. If there are any such individuals, please accept my apologies. Each and every word of encouragement and all professional and personal comments, critiques, and suggestions were gratefully received.

It is both my hope and my prayer that the liberating power of faith will enable you the readers to name your disgrace shame, embrace its reality, and overcome its debilitating and paralyzing effects, and that you find unconditional acceptance afforded by the grace of God, whose love and intention it is that your life be one of fulfillment and abiding joy.

Introduction:
Jan's Story

From all appearances and by conventional standards of evaluation, Jan would have been described as a well-balanced and healthy person. She had a college education, was married with two healthy children, and lived in a lovely home. Jan worked part-time for a local school district as a speech therapist while her husband Mike was employed as an architect for a successful firm. The family had all of the trappings of success from a financial and social point of view, but Jan often felt depressed, discouraged, and distressed about her own life. She imaged herself as a miserable failure. Despite reassurances from her spouse, family, and friends, she continued to experience the nagging feelings of emptiness, worthlessness, and a seemingly unidentifiable malaise. She felt physically tired, emotionally drained, and spiritually empty. It was difficult for her to describe her situation with any precision, but she sensed that something was radically wrong with who she was as a person.

One Sunday her pastor preached an especially fine sermon on the meaning of forgiveness and the powerful release from sin which the Gospel proclaims and promises. Jan was touched by the message and made an appointment with her pastor to share her pervasive feelings of pain about her own life. She surmised that her problem had to do with her spiritual life and that she had never really experienced the liberating power of forgiveness. She hoped that her time with the pastor would provide an occasion for true forgiveness to occur and that she would experience a new lease on life.

She discussed with her pastor some of the things that were bothering her. She remembered from her childhood a petty theft at a local candy store. There was the high school kegger and subsequent "skinny-dipping" episode. At the time of her father's death there had been a family quarrel with some of her siblings when some hateful and spiteful things were said, causing a rift in family relationships. She felt bad that she and Mike had had a difference about having their second baby and was distressed by the subsequent sense of estrangement they experienced during her second pregnancy. She admitted that she felt terribly guilty for perpetuating gossip about a neighbor at a coffee party. Her neighbor had defeated her in a local women's club election and Jan felt very spiteful about the defeat.

After Jan confessed a number of such "sins," the pastor suggested that they share together in a ritual of forgiveness and absolution. The pastor was convinced that if Jan heard and experienced a word of grace and forgiveness, perhaps those negative feelings about herself would dissipate. Jan too believed that this was what she needed and welcomed the opportunity to participate. After the session the pastor asked Jan how she felt. Her response was, "I feel worse than ever. I don't believe that I deserve to be forgiven. I wish I hadn't told you all of those things; now I'm not sure I can face you either." She tearfully ran out of the pastor's office and left the pastor confused and distressed. Both thought that they had adequately dealt with Jan's problem of guilt and that her disposition and outlook on life would be changed. Rather than feeling liberated by the declaration of forgiveness, Jan felt even worse about herself and withdrew even more into her own world of isolation and pain.

This composite scenario is not unique for those of us who are members of the Christian community. Parishioners and pastors alike often find themselves frustrated in attempting to address situations similar to that of Jan. What happens when "forgiveness doesn't seem to work"? What is it that lies behind the feelings and reactions expressed by Jan when she and her pastor felt that they had gotten to the source of the problem? What other dynamics are at work in Jan's life? Are there other alternatives for addressing the issue and situation which seems to be all too common among people?

I would like to suggest that there is dynamic operative in Jan's life other than or in addition to that of guilt. That dynamic is shame. Because in the church and in society so much attention has been given to guilt, shame has oftentimes been overlooked and has been referred to as the forgotten emotion. Conceptually guilt and shame have often been used interchangeably, as though the two experiences were basically the same. While they are often inextricably bound together, it has been my pastoral and personal experience that a differentiation between the two is necessary. Acknowledging this difference in human experience will also suggest that a different methodology and theology be employed in addressing the issues of guilt and shame in the faith community.

This book is intended primarily for people who are interested and concerned about the relationship of faith and life experience. Guilt has been a topic of central concern in the Judeo-Christian tradition. It has prompted the time-honored paradigm of confession, forgiveness, and absolution. Shame has not received the same amount of attention, yet it often is a more fundamental issue with which people within the faith community struggle. It seems imperative that a theology dealing with shame and a methodology for addressing shame issues needs to be implemented for those who suffer under the oppressive weight of a shame-based identity. The phrase "shame-based identity" will be utilized in this book to refer to persons whose fundamental self-understanding is that she or he is a person of little or no worth or value. Identity has to do with essentiality as a human being. Those who have a shame-based identity believe in their heart of hearts that in essence they are of no account, unacceptable, and unlovable. Much can be learned from the descriptive analysis provided by researchers and counselors in the psychosocial disciplines, but in order to deal holistically with people, the spiritual dimension must also be factored into the total equation. Even though the phenomenon of shame is not a new topic in the field of psychotherapy, it has received considerably more attention in the past decade from counselors who are involved in developmental and family systems theory. Its emergence was prompted by psychologist Gershen Kaufman in his book, *Shame: The Power of Caring.*[1] Subsequent to that, several other significant works have been produced among which are: Leon Wurmser's *The Mask of Shame,*[2] Susan Miller's *The Shame Experience,*[3] Fossum and Mason's *Facing Shame: Families in Recovery,*[4] Donald L. Nathanson's collection of essays by notable writers entitled, *The Many Faces of Shame,*[5] John Bradshaw's work, *Healing the Shame That Binds You,*[6] and Kaufman's latest effort, *The Psychology of Shame.*[7] In more recent years, the appearance of Ronald and Patricia Potter-

Efron's work, *Letting Go of Shame*,[8] James Harper and Margaret Hoopes' book, *Uncovering Shame*,[9] Donald Nathanson's fascinating work entitled, *Shame and Pride: Affect, Sex, and the Birth of the Self*,[10] Michael Lewis' excellent presentation in *Shame: The Exposed Self*,[11] and Lewis B. Smedes' book, *Shame and Grace*,[12] have all contributed significantly to the conversation and understanding of shame. My purpose is not to duplicate what these skilled and perceptive writers have already written, but to draw from their expertise and experience and attempt to relate it directly and concretely to the experience of people who identify themselves most specifically with the Judeo-Christian tradition.

The various dimensions of the shame experience and the concomitant dynamics associated with it will be at the heart of this book. The lines of demarcation between shame and guilt will be articulated so that the two become distinct realities. My purpose will be to address these dynamics in an integrative fashion and relate them to various tenets of the faith tradition. It is my conviction that there is inherent within the tradition a powerful word of liberation for people who are shame-bound as well as those who may be enslaved by guilt. A workable paradigm for dealing with guilt has been developed, but a similar paradigm for dealing with shame likewise needs to be created out of the substance of the tradition itself. Finally these insights need to be implemented in such a way as to promote and enrich the spiritual growth of God's people. It is hoped that this work will provide some clues as well as strategy for such implementation. Because shame is so pervasive, there is always an inherent danger of reductionism when focusing on a singular topic. My concern is not to capitalize on a "popular psychological fad" which happens to be in vogue, but rather to ponder reflectively on the implications of this neglected concept in human experience from the faith perspective. This work is not intended to be exhaustive or definitive because of the inherent limitations found in my own theology, ethnic and racial background, gender, and personal experience. Rather, it represents one person's reflections on a critically important dimension of human experience. My hope is that as a result of your reading and reflection, your own assumptions based on gender, theology, and ethnicity will be drawn into the dialogue about shame.

The fundamental theological presupposition which undergirds this book is the belief that it is God's intention, as the writer of Hebrews says, that we be free not only from sin, but from the encumbrances which weigh us down in our lives (Hebrews 12:1). This is not to suggest that the phenomenon of shame can be eradicated from our existence, for it seems to be endemic to the human condition. However, the debilitating effects of shame can be addressed in such a way by the "good news" of God's grace that those experiencing this phenomenon need not be permanently paralyzed.

It has only been in the last few years that I have personally come to terms with the impact of shame in my own life, as well as in the life of the parishioners and students whom I have attempted to serve in my ministry. Dealing with shame has been a daily experience as I have wrestled with it in my life both professionally and personally. Hopefully in the process of struggling through these issues cognitively, affectively, theologically, and spiritually, all of us may gain a more enlightened view of ourselves and others and a more comprehensive understanding of God's grace, as well as developing a more salutary way for addressing the issue of shame within the context of the faith community.

NOTES

1. Kaufman, Gershen. *Shame: The Power of Caring*. Cambridge: Schenkmen Publishing Co., 1980.
2. Wurmser, Leon. *The Mask of Shame*. Baltimore: Johns Hopkins University Press, 1981.
3. Miller, Susan. *The Shame Experience*. Hillsdale, NJ: The Analytic Press, 1985.
4. Fossum, Merle A. and Marilyn J. Mason. *Facing Shame: Families in Recovery*. New York: W.W. Norton, 1986.
5. Nathanson, Donald L. (ed.). *The Many Faces of Shame*. New York: Guilford Press, 1987.
6. Bradshaw, John. *Healing the Shame That Binds You*. Deerfield Beach, FL: Health Communications Inc., 1988.
7. Kaufman, Gershen. *The Psychology of Shame*. New York: Springer Publishing Company, 1989.
8. Potter-Efron, Ronald and Patricia. *Letting Go of Shame*. Center City, MN: Hazelden Press, 1989.

9. Harper, James and Margaret Hoopes. *Uncovering Shame*. New York: W.W. Norton and Co., 1990.

10. Nathanson, Donald. *Shame and Pride: Affect, Sex, and the Birth of the Self*. New York: W.W. Norton, 1992.

11. Lewis, Michael. *Shame: The Exposed Self*. New York: Free Press, 1992.

12. Smedes, Lewis. *Shame and Grace*. San Francisco: Harper Collins, 1993.

Chapter One

The Nature of Shame

There are a variety of perspectives from which one could deal with the issue of shame. It could be considered from a psychological, sociological, philosophical, or theological perspective. Significant literary works have been written from all of these varying perspectives. The understanding of the nature of shame is obviously shaped by the particular perspective or discipline represented.

DIALECTICAL NATURE OF SHAME

Etymologically and conceptually, shame provides its own kind of dialectic. Carl Schneider in his masterful work, *Shame, Exposure and Privacy,*[1] has made a very helpful distinction between what he terms "disgrace" shame and "discretionary" shame. He contends that preeminence has been given to disgrace shame and that discretion shame has been virtually ignored. His thesis is that,

> The contemporary rejection of shame is rooted in a faith commitment to reason, science and self-realization. This commitment, in turn is a late incarnation of the Enlightenment ideals of reason and individual autonomy. . . . The practical consequences of this ideal was a determination to remove shame from human experience in order to prove the point that reason could triumph over custom, tradition and shame and lead to human liberation.[2]

Schneider is speaking about discretionary shame when he writes about its contemporary rejection. It is his thesis that discretionary and disgrace shame must be kept in dialectical tension giving credence to both as an integral part of human experience. The preoccupation with disgrace shame has left the issue of discretionary shame forgotten in the shadows. An explication of the meaning of both faces of shame will illustrate the necessity of considering them within a dialectical framework.

DISCRETIONARY SHAME

Nineteenth-century writers such as Thomas H. Burgess, Darwin, Tolstoy, Dostoyevski, and especially Nietzsche gave credence to discretionary shame and its positive value in human interaction. Discretionary shame has the positive function of insuring a modicum of modesty, privacy, propriety, and prudence. Its function is to establish appropriate boundaries in order to guard against invasive or intrusive actions which can violate the dignity and integrity of another human being. Nathanson states it succinctly, ". . . shame guards the boundaries of the self."[3] Schneider's concern is that existence devoid of discretionary shame may preclude the establishment of a true sense of integrity and personhood.

Discretionary shame is an integral and necessary part of a healthy person's existence. Schneider sees discretionary shame as being linked primarily to modesty, which has an ethical component to it. He writes,

> The close parallel between shame and modesty, on the other hand, suggests an ethical element in shame, inasmuch as modesty is normally treated as a virtue. . . . The connection between shame and virtue is even more closely established when we note that culture regularly gives shamelessness a negative connotation. The concept of shamelessness suggests that the lack of a proper sense of shame is a moral deficiency and that the possession of shame is a moral obligation.[4]

As intimated earlier, Schneider relies heavily upon literary figures from the nineteenth century, particularly the writings of Nietzsche, to make his case for the importance of discretionary shame. Nietzsche invokes harsh invectives against Christianity as it comes to expression in the mysticism of St. Paul and criticizes its perfidiousness in the shameless adaptation of pagan practices. He accuses Christianity of shameless intellectual dishonesty as well as immodesty in its penchant for "helping others."[5] The predisposition of Christians to always "be of help" and to express sympathy to others elicited from Nietzsche an indictment of invasiveness. Nietzsche's principal concern was for the protection of the individual and the right of every person to the establishment of self-determined parameters which were not to be violated. Schneider hastens to add that Nietzsche's accusations were not only levied against Christianity, but against socialism and education as well.

Whereas modern society under the influence particularly of psychoanalytical thought has railed against the phoniness and superficiality of the masks which each of us wears, Nietzsche contended that out of a sense of discretionary shame, " 'Every profound spirit needs a mask' to protect his vulnerability."[6] The indiscriminate invasion into another's world of thoughts and feelings is not an inherent right of any human being. Schneider mounts a convincing argument for the importance of maintaining the dynamic of discretionary shame. He says, "Each of us needs some time offstage, a private space, before we are ready to go public. Rehearsal is a process which becomes more sophisticated and differentiated as we mature, but throughout life it is a human need."[7] Bradshaw uses the term "healthy" shame to encompass the same concern.[8] David Augsburger has also picked up on this same theme and explicates it in a cross-cultural context.[9] The concern registered in this discussion is for respecting the boundaries or the parameters which humans erect for their own sense of protection. To utilize another phrase often cited in the language of human rights, every person has a "right to privacy."

Perhaps some contemporary examples will serve to illustrate the importance of discretionary shame and the resultant damage when boundaries are not observed. Activities associated with sex, bodily elimination, death, and some dimensions of religious expression, as well as certain experiences of tragedy and trauma, are considered as private matters.

Our social sense of discretion precludes people from engaging in sexual activity in the public arena. Such behavior is a violation of the law and those who are caught are subject to arrest. It is not that the behavior in and of itself is unlawful, rather it is the indiscriminate exposure which is an offense to the public sense of propriety. Such "shameless" behavior constitutes a moral and legal infraction.

Discretionary shame stipulates that "indecent exposure" of any kind is a violation of the social and moral contract that prevails in our society. Exhibitionism is indicative of severe emotional problems, but it is also a violation of the law. Shame has to do with issues of "exposure" and in the eyes of the law, such behavior is considered "indecent." Sexual expression is a private, not a public, matter and those who fail to observe these parameters of propriety are considered to be "shameless" in their behavior and in violation of the law.

Conversely, since the sex act is deemed a personal and private matter between partners, it is not for public scrutiny. Voyeurism like exhibitionism may be indicative of an emotional disorder, but it is a violation of the law. It represents an invasion of privacy and the crossing of a social boundary. While most people would seek to preserve their personal privacy in matters relating to their sexual activity, prurient interests seem to prevail that constitute a kind of public voyeurism. For example, the voluminous sale of tabloids that exploit private lives, particularly of well-known public figures, is indicative of the human proclivity for violating the boundaries of discretionary shame. The lure utilized to entice the sale of such material is that inquiring minds want to know, whether or not they have a right to know.

The issues surrounding sexual harassment are primarily matters related to power as it comes to expression in sexism. On another level, sexual harassment involves a violation of personal boundaries whether it is related to touch, gestures, suggestive language, or the verbal exploitation of the sexuality of another person. Victims of sexual harassment often state that they have felt invaded and thus violated. An unwelcome intrusion upon physical and/or emotionally private space has been experienced to the detriment of the victim.

Another example of discretionary shame is the need for privacy when attending to issues involving bodily elimination. It is considered an invasion of privacy to walk into an occupied bathroom

The Nature of Shame

when the door is closed. A violation of the same may bring an angered response regarding this intrusion. People who are physically incapable of attending to their own needs relative to body elimination sacrifice a great deal of their personal sense of privacy because necessity dictates reliance upon others to meet these needs. The parameters of propriety are culturally conditioned, so it is imperative to be sensitive to the operative norms in any given setting.

The death experience is also considered to be a private matter. Intimate loved ones may be in attendance, but it is not an event that invites the curious onlooker. Carl Schneider states that "The sense of shame, therefore, protects the dying from the violation that would cause embarrassment, disgrace-shame, or humiliation."[10] We make a relatively private entrance into the world at birth and likewise feel most comfortable making a relatively private exit from the world at death. The ignominy of public executions is a prime example of the public exposure of the private experience of death. The alleged benefit of such a practice in some societies is that it serves as a deterrent to crime. In part, the rationale employed appears to be an appeal to would-be offenders that they not commit the crime because the consequences involve the horror of dying exposed to the public eye.

The human experience of devastating trauma and tragedy is likewise to be protected from exploitation by a healthy sense of discretionary shame. It is appalling to me how often those who have experienced traumatic devastation have a microphone thrust into their face and a TV camera trained on them in the midst of shock, grief, horror, and pain. The importance of the story seemingly takes precedence over any personal needs that victims may have for privacy. The cost to human dignity, integrity, and privacy is incalculable.

The religious expression of discretionary shame takes the form of "awe" and "wonder" in the presence of the holy. It is an acknowledgement of the gap and the gulf between the human and the divine. Isaiah experiences this phenomenon in his call (Isaiah 6:1-8) and Peter makes a similar confession in his experience with Jesus in Luke 5:8, wherein the acknowledged presence of the divine Peter says, "Depart from me for I am a sinful man." Human beings cannot tolerate the glory or the revealing light of God, even when it is reflected in someone else's face (Exodus 34:30, II Corinthians 3:7-18). The boundaries are established between the holy and the human even with regard to place and space (e.g., Exodus 3:5, Exodus 19:12-13, II Samuel 6:6-11). It is the kind of awe and reverence which Rudolf Otto calls the "mysterium tremendum."[11] A more contemporary expression of dealing with the issue of the mystery of God has been written by Eberhard Jungel. He asserts that the problem centers about the difficulty of the "speakability of God."[12] The only way in which human beings can speak about God is in metaphorical terms because that is the only language accessible to us. Even utilizing images and metaphors, we do not want to confuse the creature and the Creator in the process. God is God and human beings are human beings. While we may use metaphors to speak of that which is beyond human comprehension and even employ anthropomorphic language in order to provide images that are accessible, the fundamental temptation is still the desire to be like God. The conceptual medium dares not supplant or become confused with the reality that it represents. The issue is how to speak meaningfully about God without violating the boundaries. The demarcation between the divine and human has been established and is to be maintained. Discretion is to be employed when dealing with that which is holy.

Discretionary shame is a dynamic which also operates in relationship to boundaries between members of the faith community. Schneider states,

> What is inner to another may be his or her faith. Shame protects faith, and we must protect shame. The anonymous donor, the anonymous author deserve privacy lest the sentiments that animate their creative acts be inappropriately exposed and reduced by shame.[13]

This same concern for exposure is appropriate in all human relationships. Respecting the privacy of others is integral to respecting their personhood. Discretionary shame protects the person's world from disintegration. Human beings cannot exist devoid of those defenses which protect them from the invasion of others, even when the other person may mean no harm. It reminds us all that we are overstepping boundaries of others if there is any kind of coercive demand for disclosure. The relationship can deteriorate to the point of being little more than a kind of emotional voyeurism with its prodding, pushing, probing, prying, and pillaging of the human psyche. Privacy needs to be protected, modesty is to be valued, virtue and boundaries need to be guarded so that indiscriminate exposure and a violating sense of invasiveness is precluded both in life and in the experience of death. This is the value of discretionary shame. If one is to deal effectively with disgrace shame, the balance between the two must be kept in tension and the two always need to be considered in juxtaposition.

DISGRACE SHAME

Disgrace shame, in contrast to discretionary shame, can be a painfully paralyzing and debilitating experience.

If discretion shame sustains the personal and social ordering of the world, disgrace shame is a painful experience of the disintegration of one's world. A break occurs in the self's relationship with itself and/or others. An awkward, uncomfortable space opens up in the world. The self is no longer whole, but divided. It feels less than it wants to be, less than at its best it knows itself to be.[14]

The impact of this powerfully pervasive phenomenon which has been labeled by Fossum and Mason as the "invisible dragon"[15] has not only terrorized the emotional arena of human existence, but can threaten physical health and truncate developmental and spiritual growth. A further explication and delineation of these dynamics will be addressed in a subsequent chapter.

It seems obvious that the tenets of what Schneider terms discretionary shame need to be safeguarded. The negative consequences of disgrace shame need to be constructively addressed while at the same time learning from those shame feelings and experiences what they might teach us concerning human experience and existence.

Even though historically and philologically "shame" as a word has carried this dialectical or bipolar character, I wonder whether in popular parlance the word can be expected to carry the freight of this dual meaning. Perhaps because of the powerful impact of the psychoanalytical movement, the associations made with the word "shame" in our society have been reduced to its negative connotations. It may be unfortunate that this word, like others, which has such a rich meaning historically, has been emptied of its full implications by popular usage. Yet, this is the nature of a living language; it is not static, but dynamic, and is shaped by the shared meaning of the symbol in current conversation.

For the sake of clarity, the word "shame" in this book will refer to "disgrace" shame as defined by Schneider and others. When making reference to "discretionary shame," I will more often than not utilize images and words that have to do with boundaries. Privacy, propriety, prudence, and parameters are words that in contemporary usage seem to capture more adequately the nature of discretionary shame as it relates to relationships between people.

Whether one is dealing with discretionary or disgrace shame, both have in common the concern for vulnerability, disclosure, and exposure. Discretionary shame concerns itself with the protection of the private sphere of human activity so that public scrutiny is precluded. Disgrace shame on the other hand is fearful of exposure out of concern for the image of the self which others may develop should other people see the "real" me with all of my disgusting ways, deficiencies, and defects. The tension inevitably is between exposure and hiddenness. Carl Schneider makes the assertion that "shame as discretion" involves the employment of appropriate restraint for the sake of the relationship. Discretionary shame then is the governing value considered by a person *before* she or he acts. Disgrace shame, on the other hand, is the painful experience of disintegration that often *follows* a given act or circumstance.[16] The correlation between the two resides in the common denominator of exposure.

Before addressing more specifically the dynamics of disgrace shame and its relationship to human experience and spiritual life, it is imperative that its distinction from guilt be discussed. As noted earlier, even though the two are often inextricably bound together, it is helpful to make conceptual distinctions for the sake of understanding the human experience of both guilt and shame, as well as indicating the most salutary way of ameliorating them and appropriating them into the total context of human existence.

NOTES

1. Schneider, Carl D. *Shame, Exposure, and Privacy.* Boston: Beacon Press, 1977.

2. Schneider, p. 1.

3. Nathanson, Donald L. (ed.). *The Many Faces of Shame.* New York: Guilford Press, 1987, p. 46.

4. Schneider, p. 19.

5. Schneider, p. 12.

6. Schneider, p. 16.

7. Schneider, Carl D. "A Mature Sense of Shame." In Donald L. Nathanson (ed.), *The Many Faces of Shame.* New York: Guilford Press, 1987, p. 201.

8. Bradshaw, John. *Healing the Shame That Binds You.* Deerfield Beach, FL. Health Communications Inc., 1988, pp. 3-9.

9. Augsburger, David. *Counseling in a Cross-Cultural Setting.* Philadelphia: Westminster Press, 1986, pp. 11-143.

10. Schneider, *Shame, Exposure and Privacy,* p. 80.

11. Otto, Rudolf. *The Idea of the Holy.* New York: Oxford University Press, 1958, pp. 12-24.

12. Jungel, Eberhard. *God, the Mystery of the World.* Grand Rapids: Eerdmans Publishing Company, 1983. See specifically pp. 226-298.

13. Schneider. "A Mature Sense of Shame," p. 195.

14. Schneider, *Shame, Exposure and Privacy,* p. 22.

15. Fossum, Merle and Marilyn Mason. *Facing Shame: Families in Recovery.* New York: W.W. Norton, 1986, pp. 1-18.

16. Schneider, *Shame, Exposure and Privacy,* pp. 19-25.

Chapter Two

Distinctions Between Guilt and Shame

Historically in the theological, sociological, and psychological arenas the focus of attention has centered if not fixated on guilt. Since this book specifically targets the faith community, principal attention will be given to the theological and ecclesiological dimensions. Much of classical theology concerns itself with the centrality of guilt which is a result of sins of commission or omission committed by members of the community. The violation of the covenant relationship established by God and God's gracious restoration of that covenant constitutes the core of the biblical salvation story. The covenantal bond established within the community, in relationship to other communities as well as nature, has also been broken. The brokenness occasioned by sin that is a recurrent theme among early church leaders, finds an eloquent spokesperson in St. Augustine and comes most dramatically to expression in Reformation theology. Sinful acts result in ruptured relationships between God and human beings as well as disruptions in the relationships between people and with the whole created order.

An example of the effects of sin as an experience of corporate guilt can be illustrated in its systemic form when considering the ecological problem of water pollution. The irresponsible and illicit dumping of toxic waste material into our oceans, rivers, and streams has resulted in the endangerment of aquatic life. This "sin" against nature disrupts the ecological system in that certain species of aquatic life are in danger of extinction. The implications of such behavior have even more far-reaching effects. Every creature in the food chain, including human beings, is likewise threatened with illness or death. In the consumption of fish and crustaceans, the carcinogenic toxins are spread to every creature that consumes

17

these creatures as food. The deleterious effects thus spread like a contagious disease and affect the entire food chain. Disregard for the created order, whether occasioned by greed, disrespect, irresponsibility, or passivity, results in the diminishment and often demise of God's created order. It is not only those who perpetrate such acts of violence against nature who are guilty of sin. All of the rest of us who passively sit by and allow it to happen also fall under the indictment of sin and suffer the guilt of our inaction. Whether it involves the sin of commission or omission, we all stand guilty before God.

Moving from the macrocosm to the microcosm, it is not only systemic sin and its consequent guilt that plagues us, since the impact of sin and guilt in personal relationships also creates havoc in the lives of people.

To take a specific example, consider what happens when a marital infidelity results in the dissolution of a marriage relationship. It is not only the parties involved who are victimized by these often virulent relationships, but families and friends suffer as well. Smoldering anger, bitterness, resentment, and divisiveness rear their ugly heads like monsters from the deep and devour the parties involved. Sinful behavior in its systemic or corporate form, as well as in its individual manifestation, results in the experience of guilt. Ruptured and fractured relationships cut a wide path of destruction and leave a trail of debris in nature as well as in the human arena.

These fractured relationships require forgiveness, reconciliation, and restoration which is accomplished by an act of divine love and grace. Gerhard Kittel has contended that "forgiveness" constitutes the core of the Christian proclamation.[1] God's unilateral act of grace accomplishes at-one-ment which is mediated through Jesus Christ. As Gustaf Aulen has demonstrated, there is no unanimity within the biblical or ecclesiastical tradition with regard to how the atonement is to be appropriated, hence a variety of theories which attempt to capture the essence of this divine activity have been formulated.[2]

One of the fundamental understandings of guilt is that it results from a violation or transgression of the acknowledged and accepted communal or corporate code of conduct in relationship to God as well as other human beings. Violating the established precepts of moral or ethical propriety results objectively in being declared guilty and subjectively in feeling guilty. In the biblical tradition, the concern is not primarily for the individual conscience, as important as that has come to be in much of modern religion, but rather that the transgression constituted a communal breach of covenant with God and the faith community.

Two biblical examples may serve to illustrate the point of corporate guilt. The first is the narrative regarding the man Achan in the Book of Joshua, chapter seven. It was Achan who stole some of the spoil as a result of the conquest of Jericho. The writer of the story says that ". . . the people of Israel broke faith in regard to the devoted things . . ." (Joshua 7:1). As a result of Achan's disobedience, the military effort against the city of Ai failed (Joshua 7:5). As the leader of Israel, Joshua feels like he has been betrayed by God and complains bitterly before Yahweh (Joshua 7:6-9). The Divine reply is that ". . . Israel has sinned; . . ." (Joshua 7:11) with no specific mention made of Achan as sole culprit. The whole of Israel could suffer from the absence of Yahweh unless the sin of disobedience is unearthed. As a consequence, every tribe and family is brought before Joshua until such time as the guilty party is determined (Joshua 7:18-19). Achan is repentant (verses 20-21), but the purification of Israel from this abomination of disobedience is not complete until not only Achan, but his whole family and all of his possessions, are destroyed (Joshua 7:24-26).

When this narrative is read, most of us are incensed at the seeming injustice that is perpetrated, particularly upon Achan's family and flocks. What makes it even more devastating is that seemingly this is what God desires in order to accomplish justice for the misdeed and restoration for the people of Israel. Why should they all be destroyed because of one man's sin? Our rampant individualism protests vehemently against the injustice we see as being perpetrated in this narrative. The individual rights of all of Achan's family members have been violated. The concept of corporate personality prevails. The individual is not thought of apart from the group, nor the group apart from the individual. There has been a breach of the covenant via one person, but it impacts the whole nation of Israel. The closest we seem to be able to come to understanding this concept is the adage which states, "one rotten apple can spoil the whole barrel."

A second illustration comes from the fifth chapter of the Book of Acts in the New Testament. The communal covenantal agreement among these early Christians was that they were to have "... everything in common" (Acts 4:32). The sin and consequent guilt of Ananias and Sapphira was that they kept a portion of the proceeds from the sale of their personal effects (Acts 5:2). This is construed as a breach of the communal covenant that the early Christians had with God (Acts 5:4). As a result of their sin of disobedience and greed, both suffered death (Acts 5:5, 10). Once again our sensitivities are violated by this narrative. We might say, "let the punishment fit the crime!" Keeping some of the proceeds might be interpreted as a wise and prudent move. Why is this couple literally punished with death for a seemingly inconsequential act? The point of the story is that the covenant with God has been broken by their sin and consequent guilt. The whole community is endangered by such disobedience. Communal restoration is contingent on communal repentance and reparation in order that reconciliation might occur. Reconciliation with God, others, nature, and the self was imperative if harmony was to be restored. This meant that the individual or individuals responsible for the transgression were to acknowledge culpability, accept responsibility, and expect accountability for their behavior. Corporate as well as individual covenant breaking implied serious consequences.

Guilt carries its own divine and/or human consequences as determined by the gravity of the infraction. The holiness code and other apodictic and casuistic laws are examples of the communal proscriptions of the covenant community with concomitant prescriptive directives regarding the severity and implementation of justice if these laws were violated. (The Book of Leviticus in the Old Testament contains many of these "holiness" laws.) The values of the community were considered and the law was established in such a way as to have the punishment fit the crime. In the execution of the punishment or retribution for the guilty act, the purpose was not only or even primarily punitive, but rather to ensure stability within the community. The ultimate purpose in dealing directly with guilt was to hold up and deepen the moral and ethical value system of the community.

The most concrete example of the nature of guilt can be seen in any system of jurisprudence. The law is broken, violated, or transgressed. When the violator is apprehended that person is given the opportunity to admit culpability for the act and is judged as being guilty for the volitional or even inadvertent transgression of the law. The person is assessed a fine or imprisoned under the "guidelines of the law" or in some other way makes restitution for the damage occasioned by the incident. Having "paid the debt to society," the person is set free to reassume her or his role.

The biblical tradition also makes clear that there is a process whereby the guilt which is incurred as a result of sin can be dealt with within the framework of the faith tradition.

The attenuation of the guilt and the concomitant guilt feelings were accomplished by confession of the same to the party or parties offended, whether that was God or others. There was an appeal for forgiveness, an apology, and often appropriate restitution for the harm which was done. Once the established sequence was completed, the person or persons could experience forgiveness, freedom from the guilt, and reconciliation. The process resulted in the possibility of becoming reinstated in the covenant relationship with God and in the social network of the community. The Old Testament institution of sacrifice and the New Testament witness to the sacrifice of Christ have traditionally symbolized the manner in which the covenantal relationship has been reestablished.

Articulating the process utilizing theological nomenclature, one may sin against God, others, nature or self; feel the guilt of the broken relationship; make confession of that guilt, and ask for mercy and forgiveness; and receive ritual restoration through absolution. If feasible and possible, restitution or amends may be appropriate not as a kind of punishment or penance, but as an act of goodwill. Having been liberated from the judgment and consequences of guilt, the person or persons are reconciled with God, others, nature, or self and are restored to wholeness and fellowship in the faith community. Theologically, liturgically, and pastorally, this has been the normal modus operandi in the faith tradition. The assumption is that people suffer primarily from guilt and need to follow the prescribed process in order to experience the gift of forgiveness and reconciliation. The genius of the process as outlined is that it provides a way back into the life of the community.

The slate is cleared as it were and resumption of life is once again possible. God only knows how critically important this process is for those laden with guilt.

Perhaps your experience is similar to Jan's story cited earlier. There are numerous occasions in my own pastoral ministry when the distinction between guilt and disgrace shame was missed. A woman whom I shall call "Mary" made an appointment with me to talk about her feelings of uneasiness around other people. She was sure that this sensation was a result of something that she had done and she indicated that she felt guilty about avoiding gatherings. She felt particularly guilty about not socializing at congregational gatherings. While there may have been some "socialized guilt" about not attending church functions, had I pressed the issue pastorally, I suspect that I would have found the presence of "disgrace shame" and not guilt to be the real culprit in her life.

Operating with the presupposition that one is dealing primarily with guilt, the guilt-alleviating process of confession and forgiveness may be employed, but as with Jan and Mary, one may not only not experience a sense of forgiveness or relief, but may feel even worse and be plunged into greater distress and despair. When this occurs it may be indicative of the fact that the primary issue is shame and not guilt. Guilt may also be an important factor, but it is often necessary to first deal with the shame before a gracious word of forgiveness can be heard and appropriated for the guilt. Whereas guilt may be characterized phenomenologically as a behavioral violation of one's value system, shame is an ontological violation of one's essentiality or identity as a person.

Shame results in feelings of worthlessness, helplessness, and hopelessness as one feels judged by others and judges oneself as of no value, consequence, purpose, worth, or significance. The self views the self from the shame perspective and like a malignancy the shame metastasizes to permeate the entire person, physically, emotionally, socially, and spiritually. Furthermore, shame often has the malignant effect of extending its tentacles to encompass others who are related in a significant fashion to the shame-based person. Unlike guilt, where a "way back" is provided as noted earlier, the individual possessed by a shame perspective and perception believes there is no way back to the mainstream of life.

The individual feels trapped and mired in the swamp-like back-waters of existence. Or, to employ another metaphor, the person feels helplessly drawn into the vortex of a strong whirlpool which spirals inexorably downward into the watery abyss. There appears to be no established social or religious rite or ritual which can effect restoration. It is this expressed sense of "stuckness" and paralysis, of groping despairingly around in the darkness with no light at the end of the tunnel, which makes dealing with shame so difficult. The natural inclination of the shame-based person is to fearfully and anxiously hide, to cover up so that the shame will not be seen. A massive amount of energy is devoted to this process since one's whole identity is at stake.

A biblical paradigm may be helpful in making the conceptual differentiation and distinction between shame and guilt. The Genesis 3 story regarding the fall captures the dynamics of guilt and shame very well. The command or law (moral or ethical precept) not to eat of the forbidden fruit was violated by disobedience, thus issuing in a proper sense of guilt and a feeling of being guilty. If one were to analyze this text further, the deeper issue behind the disobedience is the lack of trust that Adam and Eve had in God. As the narrative points out, they could not trust God to be God and so it was their desire to be like God! Lack of trust in God and the desire to usurp the place of God and thus confuse the Creator and the creature appears to be a condition endemic to human experience.

There are many instances in which guilt is the predominant player in human experience. When one is convicted of breaking the law or when there has been a conscious awareness of a violation of one's ethical standards or the breach of a person's moral values guilt takes front and center stage. The guilt associated with "doing" something wrong can quickly turn into a sense of shame about my "being" as a person. In the Genesis 3 story, the guilt did not prompt an honest confession of the transgression with a resultant possibility for forgiveness and restitution; rather the guilt turned into shame and the principal concern was an anxious and fearful hiding from view. The nakedness which required covering does not represent discretionary shame which protected the privacy of their sexuality; rather they feared exposure of themselves and the character of their inmost essentiality as persons. The juxtaposition of guilt and shame in this story would fall into the category of "guilty shame" as delineated by David Augsburger.[3] His categories of disgrace shame are similar to my own categories which will be explored in the next chapter.

They needed to first process their shame issues before they could constructively deal with their guilt. Likewise many of us who are members of the faith community must first deal with the isolating barriers and walls of shame before a gracious word of forgiveness can be appropriated for our guilt. When shame and guilt are confused or conceptually understood as synonymous, the ritual of confession, forgiveness, and absolution for a person's guilt misses the point and will only exacerbate the sense of shame as it did with Jan in our opening story. The two phenomena are different and must be dealt with accordingly. Even if the two are inextricably bound together as in the Genesis story, and as is so often the case with people today, the two must be dealt with separately in order to facilitate healing. The relevant theological foundations and methodological processes are determined by whether one is dealing with the dynamics of guilt or shame.

The theological distinctions are paralleled in the psychosocial arena as well. Susan Miller says that,

> Shame and guilt often co-occur, and they hold certain elements in common. Due to these shared features, shifts between the states occur rapidly and conceptual boundaries between the feeling-categories are difficult to maintain. Shame and guilt are most similar and most easily confused when moral shame is the type in question. Shame over ineffectiveness (as opposed to shame over immorality) generally is well distinguished from guilt. In fact, the clear differences between shame and guilt when shame involves no moral issues may explain the common conviction that shame and guilt are different states even though they are sometimes hard to distinguish.[4]

The behavior-being distinctions prevail also in the conceptual schema of those whose primary concern is the psychodynamics of the experience. "Experience teaches us that wrongdoing may be punished by guilt; while unwarranted opinions about the self, when exposed, will be punished by shame."[5] Shame involves more the issues of self-consciousness and self-imaging than is the case with guilt. "The experience of shame is directly about the self, which is the focus of a negative evaluation. In guilt, it is the thing done or undone that is the direct focus of negative evaluation."[6] Human capability enables the person not only to experience the shame, but to sense that others can "see" what is going on inside the person at this point in time.

Michael Lewis does an extraordinarily fine job in making clear the distinction between guilt and disgrace shame. He cites an observation made by Darwin and summarizes it in this manner.

> He [Darwin] saw guilt as regret over some fault committed; a person's relationship to others could then turn that guilt into shame. So, for example, he pointed out that one can feel guilty in solitude but would not blush because it is not the guilt over an action, but what others think or know about our own guilt which leads to the blushing [shame]. He did note that a blush might occur in solitude, but only because we might be thinking about what others might be thinking of us. Again, the opinions of others about our appearance, especially the appearance of our faces, or our conduct, are Darwin's elicitors of shame.[7]

The perspective that Lewis employs in making his own contribution to the psychosocial theory of distinguishing shame and guilt has to do with the phenomenon of "interruption" in the course of human experience. Lewis states,

> The difference between shame and guilt resides in the nature of the interruption. In guilt, the command is essentially "Stop. What you are doing violates the standard or rule. Pay attention to what you did and alter your behavior." Guilt is designed to alert the organism that the behavior violates some rule or standard in order to alter that behavior. Its function is to alert or to provoke anxiety. In addition, it directs behavior toward alternative action patterns that repair the inappropriate behavior that has been called into question.
>
>   In shame the command is much more severe: "Stop. You are no good." More important, it is about self, not about action; thus, rather than resetting the machine toward action, it

stops the machine. Any action becomes impossible since the machine itself is wrong. The shame interruption is more intense given the identity of the subject-object. That the violation involves the machine itself means, functionally, that all behavior ceases. Its function, then, is to signal the avoidance of behaviors likely to cause it. Its aversiveness functions to ensure conformity to the standards and rules.[8]

The research done by Lewis eventuates in his tendering definitions for disgrace shame and guilt. The conceptual distinctions are exceedingly helpful and warrant being quoted in their entirety.

Shame is the product of a complex set of cognitive activities: the evaluation of an individual's actions in regard to her standards, rules, and goals, and her global evaluation of the self. The phenomenological experience of the person having shame is that of a wish to hide, disappear, or die. Shame is a highly negative and painful state that also results in the disruption of ongoing behavior, confusion in thought, and an inability to speak. The physical action accompanying shame includes a shrinking of the body, as though to disappear from the eye of the self or the other. This emotional state is so intense and has such a devastating effect on the self system that individuals presented with such a state must attempt to rid themselves of it. However, since shame represents a global attack on the self, people have great difficulty in dissipating this emotion. . . .

The emotional state of guilt or regret is produced when individuals evaluate their behavior as failure but focus on the specific features of the self or on the self's action that led to the failure. Unlike shame, in which the focus is on the global self, with guilt the individual focuses on the self's actions and behaviors that are likely to repair the failure. From a phenomenological point of view, individuals are pained by their failure, but this pained feeling is directed to the cause of the failure or to the harmed object. Because the cognitive attributional process focuses on the action of the self rather than on the totality of the self, the feeling that is produced is not as intensely negative as shame and does not lead to confusion and to the loss of action. In fact, the emotion of guilt always has an associated corrective action, something that the individual can do–but does not necessarily actually do–to repair the failure. Rectification of the failure and preventing it from happening again are the two possible corrective paths.[9]

The definitions and exposition of the dynamics of guilt and shame from the psychosocial perspective parallel the process outlined from the biblical and theological perspective.

Nathanson conceptualizes the differences between shame and guilt in spatial categories. Quoting Leon Wurmser in substantiating this point he says, "Wurmser (1981) has explained, the difference between shame and guilt is that shame guards the boundaries of the self, while with guilt we have taken action and aggressed on the territory of another."[10] In that sense guilt can be equated with behavioral transgression while shame is more closely associated with the violation or invasion of one's being. John Patton summarizes it in this fashion, "Guilt can more nearly be dealt with according to rational principle, whereas shame is inevitably relational and personal."[11]

One could cite other theorists as well as therapists who find the behavior-being distinction an important one in sorting out the dynamics of guilt and shame from a therapeutic perspective. The basic point of the discussion is to demonstrate the fact that the distinctions which are made from a theological perspective are in concert with those discovered by the social sciences. As one attempts to deal holistically with people and to take into account the totality of their existence as it comes to expression in body, mind, emotions, and spirit; the distinction between guilt and shame serves us well in this endeavor.

NOTES

1. Kittel, Gerhard (ed.). *Theological Dictionary of the New Testament,* Vol 1. Grand Rapids: W. B. Eerdman Company, 1964, pp. 509-512.

2. Aulen, Gustaf. *Christus Victor.* New York: The Macmillan Company, 1961.

3. Augsburger, David. *Pastoral Counseling Across Cultures.* Philadelphia: Westminster Press, 1986, p. 117.

4. Miller, Susan. *The Shame Experience.* Hillsdale, MN: The Analytic Press, 1985, p. 140.

5. Nathanson, Donald L. (ed.). *The Many Faces of Shame.* New York: The Guilford Press, 1987, pp. 4-5.

6. Lewis, Michael. *Shame: The Exposed Self.* New York: Free Press, 1991, p. 30.

7. Lewis, Michael, p. 35.

8. Lewis, Michael, pp. 75-76.

9. Lewis, Helen Block. "Shame and the Narcissistic Personality." In Nathanson (ed.), *The Many Faces of Shame.* New York: Guilford Press, 1987, p. 107.

10. Nathanson, p. 260.

11. Patton, John. *Is Human Forgiveness Possible?* Nashville: Abingdon Press, 1985, p. 39.

Chapter Three

The Dynamics of Shame

Shame is an elusive phenomenon. Each person, family, community, culture, and society may use the word and its cognates in a variety of contexts. The focus of attention in this chapter will be to discuss the dynamics of disgrace shame as it is experienced in a contemporary Caucasian community. Even with that qualification, it is difficult to provide a precise definition or description of the shame experience since it is nuanced differently depending upon a multiplicity of factors which are present in any given situation. A sampling of a few definitions will illustrate the multifaceted nature of disgrace shame. Fossum and Mason state,

> Shame is an inner sense of being completely diminished or insufficient as a person. It is the self judging the self. A moment of shame may be humiliation so painful or an indignity so profound that one feels one has been robbed of her or his dignity or exposed as basically inadequate, bad, or worthy of rejection. A pervasive sense of shame is the ongoing premise that one is fundamentally bad, inadequate, defective, unworthy, or not fully valid as a human being.[1]

Schneider says that disgrace shame is a ". . . painful experience of the disintegration of one's world. A break occurs in the self's relationship with itself and/or others. An awkward, uncomfortable space opens up in the world. The self is no longer whole, but divided. It feels less than it wants to be, less than at its best it knows itself to be."[2] In using the category of toxic shame to talk about disgrace shame, Bradshaw states that it is a ". . . pervasive sense that I am flawed and defective as a human being."[3] Kaufman prefers to define shame in terms of the existential experience of its effects. He writes,

To feel shame is to feel seen in a painfully diminished sense. The self feels exposed both to itself and to anyone else present. It is this sudden unexpected feeling of exposure and accompanying self-consciousness that characterizes the essential nature of the affect of shame. Contained in the experience of shame is the piercing awareness of ourselves as fundamentally deficient in some vital way as a human being. To live with shame is to experience the very essence or heart of the self as wanting.[4]

The varying definitions all seem to focus either on the issue of exposure or the consciousness on the part of the self as being different in comparison to others. Both dynamics eventuate in a negative self-evaluation.

What may induce shame in one person, community, or culture may be nonshaming in another setting. The determination is contingent upon the social milieu and the mores which are normative in a given setting. Likewise, there appear to be varying layers or levels of shame and the degree of intensity differs widely. It may be a passing experience of little consequence or it may be an earth-shattering experience which cuts to the core of a person's existence. As we shall see, it has not only an individualistic aspect to it, but is found in families as well as larger social groupings and even nations.

Most researchers agree that shame is among the earliest experiences of human beings. Kaufman contends that the genesis of shame is experienced in the breaking of the interpersonal bridge.[5] The initial experience of disgrace shame occurs early in life when the child is given the message either through attitude or action that s/he is not wanted. Given the imperfect nature of human beings, one could say that the shame experience is an inevitability for every child born into the world. The interpersonal bridge is broken in a variety of ways as the child experiences a relational environment which is fraught with ambiguity and anxiety. Erik Erikson, in his schema of epigenetic development of humans, links it specifically to the second stage of development. He links shame with the development of self-consciousness and indicates that it behaviorally manifests itself quite early in the child's ". . . impulse to bury one's face, or to sink, right then and there into the ground."[6] Erikson believes that shame becomes rage turned against the self which results in the fantasy of wishing or desiring invisibility. It is first encountered as a force which comes from the external world. "Shame on you" is an indictment of unacceptability, the impact of which is affectively experienced by the young child through the timbre and tone of the voice long before the child has any cognitive understanding of the words. From infancy the learning of shame is more caught than taught as the child is shaped by the norms of her or his social matrix.

The shame messages from the external world become internalized and the person is molded accordingly. Thus shame can be a powerful factor in coercing conformity to prescribed social expectations which do not necessarily have a moral or ethical component to them.

The genesis of shame initially is external in origin as the child receives messages from the outside world about her or his acceptability. With the developmental process, it can be triggered internally as the young person matures and begins the task of establishing an identity through self-evaluation in relationship to significant others in life, particularly parents, peers, and others who exercise any kind of power in relationship to the developing person. Kaufman asserts that this is the way in which a shame-based identity is developed.[7]

This fascinating socialization process, termed symbolic interaction by George Herbert Mead,[8] is seen as shared symbols and experiences are interpreted in the light of meanings which are developed by the generalized other and then incorporated into the individual's own self-understanding. Identity and the sense of self-worth and value are externally referented, but with the development of the person these messages become internally appropriated. With the shame system being established and constantly refined by the social interactions of the developing person, its power begins to subtly shape the identity of the individual. The person then soon learns that it is a power not only used by others for the purpose of control, but that she/he can also attempt to use it in manipulating others.

Wurmser has made a helpful contribution in understanding shame by distinguishing between shame anxiety, shame reaction, and shame attitude.[9] Shame anxiety is an anticipatory experience. Having already experienced the pain of shame through some prior experience, one's anxiety is considerably heightened by the possibility that the experience may be duplicated. Human capability for that kind of projection concerning what might happen and the ability to envision the future can become a great source of anxiety according to Wurmser. Second, there is also the shame reaction, which is the processing of the shame event once it has made an impact upon the person. If shame anxiety is related to what might happen, the shame reaction is the result of what is happening. It is the existential encounter with the shaming situation precipitating a defensive reaction within the person since the threshold for the toleration of shame in most human beings is limited. Third, with the multiplication of shame experiences, individuals may develop a shame attitude. All of life is seen through and from the shame perspective and is lived accordingly. The individual's perception and interpretation of life experiences are governed by the attitude which arises out of a shame identity. The vicious cycle of shame is set in motion and increases in intensity with the concurrent centripetal and centrifugal forces pulling mercilessly at the very fabric of a person's being.

Susan Miller has provided a helpful historical survey of the way in which the shame experience has been interpreted from the psychological perspective. Opinion is divided as to whether shame is a direct expression of a concern or whether it functions as a disguise which is symptomatic of other problems.[10] Rather than rehearse in detail the varying psychological perspectives, I would encourage those readers who have a particular interest in reviewing the literature in psychology to the succinct synopsis provided by Miller.[11] The division in interpretation is often related to a content-versus-function posture. Is it the shame experience itself which needs specific attention (content) or is it a matter of understanding what precipitates the shame reaction (function) which requires consideration? Obviously the two perspectives are not mutually exclusive. Miller's review clearly points out that one's psychological perspective and understanding of the human situation by and large is determinative of the way in which shame is viewed, processed, and understood.

In processing shame issues with counselees and in coming to terms with my own shame, two common themes emerge which need to be noted before looking specifically at particular dynamics. It is almost universally agreed that shame is inextricably linked with exposure. Etymologically this link is noted in this manner.

The very word shame is derived from an Indo-European root (skam or skem) which means "to hide," and from which also we derive our words skin and hide, the latter in both of its meanings: the hide which covers us naturally, and that within which we seek cover. We learn to hide first for the sake of shame, and later for protection from physical danger.[12]

The fear of exposure implies that something has been hidden which if revealed would result in some form of rejection. It signals the fact that the person would feel diminished in the eyes of others, and certainly in her or his own eyes. Even the anticipation of possible shaming pushes people to extraordinary lengths to keep something secret or hidden. The experience of exposure, ". . . implies a coming into awareness of what was formerly hidden as well as a wish to hide or avoid."[13] Thus it can be said that ". . . at its core, shame is intimately linked to the human need to cover that which is exposed."[14]

The entree into the very core of the person's being in many societies is through the eyes. It is what makes prolonged eye contact an uncomfortable experience.

Shame is about eye contact. We lower our eyes, avert our gaze when embarrassed. This certainly interrupts whatever had been going on between the participants. The act of hiding from the shaming stimulus may represent an attempt to escape from the experience, to pretend it never happened. But it does more than that. The eyes are the window of the brain, and in the language of primary process, we may feel people can look in on our thoughts almost as well as we can see out. It is as if when we avert our eyes we hope to prevent the other person from knowing what we are thinking.[15]

The eyes become the presumed medium of revelation of one's inner being, thoughts, and feelings. The face often becomes the expression of the inner being and so both the eyes and the face are often covered as a protective measure against shame. Whether one is dealing with discretionary shame in which boundaries are established to ensure privacy and maintain propriety which are not to be violated through exposure or whether one is dealing with disgrace shame where the need is to remain hidden for fear of being seen, exposure is a key element in both faces of shame. The important role of the eyes, the face, or one's whole countenance in many religious traditions is immediately obvious. The Scriptures are replete with references to the role of the eyes, the face, and the countenance as revealers of a person's inner being.

The impact of cultural socialization certainly needs to be taken into account. The aversion to prolonged eye contact in our culture appears to be the fear of another seeing into the inward self. There are some societies in which any eye contact is indicative of a sign of disrespect. In those situations the issue is a culturally conditioned response to a social norm and not necessarily a manifestation of disgrace shame, though it might be of interest to investigate the historical development of such social norms.

The second dynamic which is generally operative in disgrace shame is the perception or experience of being labeled as different. This may be externally imposed by the social setting, it may be a self-designation arising out of one's own self-perception or it may be a combination of the two. The amalgamation and internalization of all messages become the normative criteria for self-evaluation. Shame arises when the evaluative process results in a person's believing and feeling that she/he is being deemed as having deviated from what is normative and as a result feels different. Even our language betrays this aspect of shame as no one wants to hear these words, "She or he is really different!" Despite all of the rhetoric about individualism and individuation and being one's own person, the fear of being labelled as abnormal, a freak, misfit, or some other pejorative epithet carries a powerful impact. Nathanson suggests that, "One of the ways those with established power preserve their hegemony is to declare themselves normative, and all others less than normal."[16]

These two prevailing dynamics really work in tandem in exacerbating the shame experience. It is usually some kind of self-perception which necessitates hiding in order that whatever might be "different" about the person should not be discovered or exposed. If discovered, the need to hide and cover up is even more pronounced, which increases the feeling that one is not normal. There is the fear of being set apart as different socially. Yet, interestingly enough, this is the core meaning of the word holy. Holy people, places, and spaces are those arenas of life which have been set apart for a specific function or purpose. Whereas the biblical witness can speak of the setting apart as a blessing, when it is appropriated in the social context, it is often experienced as a curse by those whose "set apartness" is not for the sake of distinction but discrimination. Shame appears to be the universal curse which plagues and paralyzes humankind and it comes to expression in a variety of dynamics.

DISGUST WITH THE SELF

Perhaps the most universal experience of shame comes from feeling disgusted, disappointed, or disillusioned with oneself. It may be evoked by any social faux pas or blunder which we make or any circumstance in which we end up feeling silly, stupid, or foolish. The humiliation which results from experiencing this kind of exposure results in a sense of embarrassment and a desire to hide and not be seen. Some examples from the Scriptural tradition illustrate the point well. Even though the point of the parable in Luke 14:7-11 has to do with the issue of humility, it is an example of the shame of humiliation occasioned by a social blunder. When it is discovered and then disclosed before all that the guest who assumed a place at the head table now has to make room for another, then the person ". . . will begin with shame to take the lowest place" (14:9). It makes that person look foolish and humiliation is the result. Further, in the same chapter in the parable of the building of the tower (Luke 14:28-30), the point is poignantly made that one needs to count the cost lest if you begin and are not able to finish the project, ". . . all who see it begin to mock him, saying, 'This man began to build, and was not able to finish.'" The result is a sense of humiliation and embarrassment because the exposure of one's own foolishness becomes a matter of public mockery and ridicule. The embarrassment occasioned by the shortage of wine at the wedding in Cana (John 2) is another such instance where shame is experienced as public humiliation and embarrassment issuing in feelings of disgust, disappointment, or disillusionment that more care was not taken in planning and preparation.

No one likes to look foolish, silly, or stupid, particularly in a public setting where the possibility of being laughed at or ridiculed is a present reality. We often shame ourselves internally when we catch ourselves in such a situation. Having it publicly exposed exacerbates the feeling of disgust for the self. It is as though we should have had more control over the situation and not allowed ourselves to come off looking so foolish.

More often than not, there is no moral component in these situations which would induce guilt, but rather a sense of shame and subsequent disgust elicited often by nonmoral considerations. As a former teacher of mine used to so aptly describe it, all of us are disgustingly human. Each of us wishes to make a good impression on others and have them think well of us as people. Karen Horney wrote extensively about the relationship between the ideal image of oneself and the actual or real self.[17] When a disparity exists between our ideal image of ourselves which we wish to present to others and our actual experience in a concrete situation, shame is experienced and is expressed as the discomfort or disease of embarrassment. This aspect of shame is defined as ". . . conscious or unconscious, caused by a discrepancy between expectancy and realization; an inner or an outer discrepancy, an inner or an outer conflict. It is the polarity, the tension, between how I want to be seen and how I am."[18] Miller points out that, "Some people are willing to say they feel embarrassed, because they regard embarrassment as trivial, but they are not willing to say they feel ashamed because that labeling implies for them that they are in fact shameful or defective."[19]

Any situation that renders a person vulnerable to possible public humiliation, particularly when the person may feel that the situation was preventable, may result in an experience of shame. The experience is related to loss of mastery and control over the circumstances with the added fear that one will be laughed at, held up to derision, poked fun at, or rejected. The following scenarios may be illustrative of this kind of shame with a wide spectrum of experiences included. It is important to keep in mind that such experiences are conditioned by the context and culture in which they occur.

A public speaker rises to deliver a lecture or speech and discovers that her slip is showing or his pants are unzipped. The speaker feels truly "exposed" and is disgusted with him/herself for being so careless. It was a preventable situation and the speaker's shame arises out of disgust for him/herself resulting in a desire to disappear or hide in order to escape the pain of such a public faux pas which makes that person look foolish. Another person may experience a memory lapse and succumb to stage fright because the magnitude of the moment feels so overwhelming. The comment often is that "I was mortified!!" Or the memory lapse may be forgetting a person's name after just having been introduced. This is *not* the kind of image we wish to present, nor is it the kind of thing we want others to remember about us, so we feel a great deal of shame for "blowing it" and looking and feeling so foolish.

A personal anecdote always comes to mind when thinking about shame as disgust with oneself. As a graduate student in West Germany several years ago, I was asked to give a public presentation to a local congregation about church life in America. I was anxious about my presentation, about the quality of my German pronunciation and I was determined to make a good impression. As I walked to the pulpit to address the congregation, I was so intent on what I was going to say and do that I failed to see the plexiglass hymnboard which was swung out from the wall displaying the hymn numbers and psalm for the day. I walked directly into the board and only as I heard the clatter of the little tin numbers around my ears and on the floor did I realize what was happening. I had made an impression alright, physically in my skull as evidenced by a superficial laceration, but that pain was negligible compared to the psychic pain of looking like a fool in front of all of those people. To say that I was embarrassed is to put it mildly. I felt ashamed and wanted to run away and hide and not have to face anyone because the impression I felt I left was exactly contrary to that which I had intended.

Like some other men in midlife, I try to jog daily to maintain some semblance of fitness. On occasion I drift off into my own kind of reverie and have been jarred back to reality by a solid encounter with *terra firma*! Instinctively my first reaction is *not* concern for any fractures, lacerations, or abrasions; rather I look around to see who may have seen this midlife klutz take a tumble. It is bad enough that an internal sense of shame is set off by the inability to put one foot ahead of the other, but the anxiety of exposure and others having visual evidence of my clumsiness elicits an even greater sense of shame concerning my lack of coordination.

The vocal or instrumental musician who drops a "clunker" in the midst of a performance, the athlete who makes a mistake in competition, the chef whose culinary capability is called into question because of a "flop," and the instructor who is victimized by a spoonerism or a "Freudian slip" are but a few more examples of the experience of shame which results in a sense of embarrassment because of the disparity between the image which one wishes to present and the reality of what may actually happen. The examples are legion and many of them are trivial in nature, yet issue in disgust with the self for looking foolish, particularly when the situation could have been prevented. It is particularly painful if the exposed faux pas is the occasion for finger pointing, derisive laughter, snickering, muffled conversation, head shaking, or any of a myriad of other signs and symbols that one is labeled as being silly, stupid, inept, clumsy, foolish, or some other negative evaluation.

For people with strong egos, the situation may be mitigated by humor, chalked up to human frailty, and easily dismissed; but for others with more fragile egos, the experience may drive that person deeper into seclusion and isolation. Loss of confidence, courage, self-esteem, and worth may literally fracture the fragile ego and the sense of disgust with the self may be exacerbated to the point that the person may never again want to risk again any kind of public appearance because of the possible embarrassment and humiliation occasioned by shame. Ironically, the pain of the shame is often directly proportional to the triviality of the situation which occasions it. Once the individual's identity is established as a "shameful person," it takes very little to trigger the shame mechanism.

Shame can be occasioned not only by exposure of one's failings as a human being, but also in the experience of success. When shame is associated with success and achievement, it often is mitigated by false modesty, but more often by some kind of display of anger on the part of the person. Have you ever congratulated a person for achievement and received a cold retort? The fear on the part of such people appears to be the threat of exposure whereby someone may take advantage of them. Or the fear may be that even more will be expected of them in the future as a result of the present accomplishment. The very anticipation of a possible shame situation wherein expectations may possibly exceed capability and thus make the person appear foolish is a powerful factor which may prompt self-denigration. Whereas many people will bask in the sunlight of success, the shame-based person will often seek the security of the shadows. For them success is at best accidental and at worst a threat that even more will be demanded or expected of them in the future. Denial, disavowal, and disclaimers often betray the existence of shame in the person who has difficulty dealing with success.

Those of us who are members of the faith community are particularly vulnerable to feeling foolish if some perceived flaw is evident in our life of faith. As clergy, we fear not being able to answer questions of faith posed by parishioners or we experience the anxiety of not having the right answer. These situations can evoke powerful experiences of shame. As parishioners, we do not want to look foolish in the eyes of our pastor, priest, or fellow parishioner. We strive to present an acceptable image of who we are in our faith walk. Our obsession with the fear of looking foolish in relationship to faith and our need to live perfectly can issue in emotional collapse.[20] The shame-based person is victimized by a convoluted and distorted understanding of the sanctified Christian life. In terms of the faith tradition, the person does not stand in need of forgiveness for the breach of any moral or ethical norm per se, yet the individual's sense of self has been seriously shaken and the disgust may drive the person into isolation and depression. Another perspective is needed and another healing approach necessary because what is being dealt with is disgrace shame and not guilt.

DEFICIENCY IN ONE'S PERSON

Many of the biblical references regarding the reticence of those called by God to leadership or prophetic roles is indicative of shame experienced as deficiency. Moses is convinced that he is not adequate for the task of being the liberator of God's people. He says, "Who am I that I should go to Pharaoh, and bring the people of Israel out of Egypt?" (Exodus 3:31). Moses' own sense of deficiency as a leader, particularly against overwhelming odds, would eventually reveal the fact that he was inadequate. Gideon as an appointed judge and liberator of Israel has the same plea (Judges 6:7-32). He puts the Lord to the test regarding his appointment as judge lest it eventuate in the shame of not being up to the task. Solomon's awareness of his own inadequacies prompted him to pray for wisdom as a leader so that his decisions as king would not betray his own immaturity. He says, ". . . I am but a little child; I do not know how to go out or come in. . . . Give thy servant therefore an understanding mind to govern thy people, that I may discern between good and evil; for who is able to govern this thy great people" (I Kings 3:7, 9).

There are the reluctant prophets such as Amos, Jonah, and Jeremiah who attempt to mount convincing arguments against their selection as prophets of God, citing a variety of reasons related to a sense of deficiency or inadequacy. Deficiency is often associated with age and immaturity. The injunction to young Timothy in the pastoral epistle is ". . . let no one despise your youth" (I Timothy 4:12). The accusation of immaturity, incompetence, and inexperience can have a disastrous effect. The price often paid for not measuring up to expectations is to be laughed at and scorned. The vacuum in leadership in various quarters of society may be occasioned in part by a lack of confidence. When we begin to measure ourselves against others, we come up deficient and label ourselves as inferior.

Alfred Adler identified the disgrace shame of deficiency and termed it the "inferiority complex."[21] Nathanson states that this insightful perception on the part of Adler requires a lot of attention in relationship to the shame issue.[22] Measuring oneself against others and finding oneself wanting ushers in a sense of shame for being deficient. This feeling comes to expression as a sense of inadequacy. Whereas disgust with the self is related to the inability to live up to one's idealized image, the shame of deficiency is related to the inadequacy of a person's expected capability.

The shame once again is related to both external as well as internal expectations. Kaufman indicates that expectations can be terribly disabling particularly when measured over against our perceived capabilities.[23] Each of us makes evaluative assessments of our capabilities. We may tell ourselves intellectually that we cannot be good at everything, yet the assumption we operate with emotionally is often the opposite. There arises a gnawing sense of inadequacy and a feeling of inferiority which we may attempt to hide for fear of recriminations or rejection if our inadequacy is revealed. When this shame dynamic holds sway, we fear not so much being "bad" as we succumb to the fear of not being "good" enough. An attempt to hide the inadequacy and the sense of inferiority may prompt some people to pretend or fake their way through situations. The dread, of course, is always the anxiety of being found out.

The experience of shame as deficiency may be illustrated in a number of ways. It may be gender-related, as certain assumptions are made about knowledge and competency which are related to whether one is a female or male. The socialization process for females is such that they may feel the shame of inadequacy if they are not conversant with the latest theories in child rearing or in the management of domestic affairs. Interest and capability may reside in other areas, but the social expectation is that female expertise has to do primarily with the care of children and the elderly as well as having homemaking skills. Fortunately the pressure of this stereotypical social expectation is being reduced thanks to the consciousness-raising efforts of the feminist movement. Nonetheless, oftentimes just being female in a patriarchal society issues in what Anne Wilson Schaef has termed "the original sin of being born female."[24]

Sexual stereotyping of males has a similar parallel. Males are expected to be mechanical, to work with their hands, and to display competency in those areas which historically have been assigned to males by social convention. A great deal of my own personal sense of shame is lodged in this precise point. I can vividly recall the pain of growing up and not having gifts to do even the most simple and menial mechanical tasks. Adulthood has not solved that problem. I have no more mechanical aptitude or capability now than before. I am particularly self-conscious about that when I am around others who have such skills. If I ask questions I betray my ignorance. The puzzled look, the shaking of the head, the smirk, and the body and verbal language of disbelief registered by many serves only to substantiate the feeling of inferiority and exacerbates the sense of shame. The feeling which incompetency evokes is that I am a worthless and stupid person, not worthy to be taking up space if I cannot solve the simplest of mechanical problems. "Shame on you. How can you make it in the world? Are you a man or just a wimp?" Some try to assist in ameliorating the pain by saying, "Well, you have gifts in other areas." While that may be true, the fact remains that the sexist orientation still in place in our society dictates what is really male and hence what really gives males worth often is not associated with whatever personal gifts I may possess. "You are not mechanical, therefore you are not a real male, you are inadequate and deficient . . . shame on you!" The shame experience of deficiency engenders and elicits envy of others.[25] The conscious awareness of the envy only increases the self-loathing and self-hatred. Whether the expectations are external or internal, they are a constant reminder of one's deficiency.

Thus shame as a sense of deficiency may pivot about inadequacies which are associated with stereotypical gender expectations, occupational expectations, social expectations, or any other arena in life where one does not measure up but is found to be inadequate or deficient. The result of one's not measuring up issues in the feeling of being small or diminished. As a result of being inadequate people often respond by saying, "that makes me feel so small." The constant external as well as internal messages become assimilated into one's identity. With such a concentration on the negative, the person soon becomes pegged and labelled as deficient. The stigma which is attached becomes integrated into the person as the individual begins to believe it and live it. The shame-based person is the result.[26]

DESERTION OR ABANDONMENT SHAME

The lament of the psalmist is laced with fear and trepidation in the screaming cry, "My God, my God, why have you forsaken me?" (Psalm 22:1). There is an overarching concern in the Scriptural witness that God will desert, forsake, give up on, and abandon individuals or the people as a whole. The fear of desertion among the people as a whole may be occasioned by disobedience. If we disobey God, God will desert us and forsake us. The interpretation of prevailing circumstances often leads the people to speculate whether or not God may indeed be deserting them in view of what is transpiring. It is a matter of great consequence when God threatens to desert the people (e.g., II Kings 21:14, Isaiah 2:6, Jeremiah 7:29). God is Creator, Redeemer, and Lord who has established a covenant relationship with the people and the threat of God abandoning the covenant and deserting the people threatens their whole existence. The contemplation of desertion by God in and of itself strikes terror into the heart. God is the source of life and God's presence is required to go on living.

There is not only the corporate concern, but that voiced also by individuals. The psalmist pleads with God, "Hide not thy face from me. Turn not thy servant away in anger, thou who hast been my help. Cast me not off, forsake me not, O God of my salvation!" (Psalm 27:9). The writer goes on to verbalize the reality of abandonment in his personal relationships. He says, "For my father and my mother have forsaken me. . ." (Psalm 27:10). This is the epitome of pain in human relationships, the desertion by parents, loved ones, or friends. The loneliness which is experienced is excruciating, but even more painful is the interpretation of what that desertion means, namely that no one cares and no one loves me. I have been deserted and abandoned, left without recourse or hope. Being deserted or abandoned means being separated from the source of life and love. The story of God's people, both in their corporate and individual existence, is a fear of desertion. Hence the pleas and prayers that God will not abandon us or be separated from us.

Otto Rank in his assessment of the human condition pointed to the anxiety occasioned by separation.[27] The anxiety of separation in Rank's theory begins with expulsion from the womb and all subsequent experiences wherein an individual may be left alone. Desertion or abandonment may also send a message to the person that she/he is not good enough to warrant the attention or concern of other people. This kind of dynamic plays powerfully on a person's sense of value and worth, which says to that person or group of persons, "You are not worth bothering about, you deserve nothing more than to be abandoned, deserted, and left desperately alone."

Desertion or abandonment sends a clear and frightening signal of rejection. The message of unworthiness attacks one's sense of being. If one's presence is loathsome, the conclusion drawn by that person is that I am not worthy of relationships with others and I am ashamed of myself and who I am as an individual. The message may be externally given, but is also an internal judgment made by that person. The fear of desertion and abandonment is a powerful dynamic in shaping self-perception.

This dynamic of disgrace shame appears early in life. Nathanson suggests that ". . . shame has to do with separation anxiety, the emotion calling to the attention of the child that he or she is in danger because the mothering, protecting person is unavailable."[28] The sheer panic exhibited by a child when a parent leaves for an evening out is a powerful witness to the fear of abandonment. The security of presence is the flip side of the terror of desertion. The problems experienced by some children who have been adopted relates to this primal experience of shame as abandonment. Why did my parent or parents abandon me? What's wrong with me that I was not wanted? For the young child who does not understand the reality of death, the death of a parent or parents can be experienced as desertion. Why did Mommy or Daddy die; didn't they like me?

This kind of shame may be employed by parents in an attempt to control their children. "If you do not shape up, I am going to go away and never come back." "You are so awful, I don't ever want to see you again." "If things don't change I'm going to send you away forever." Out of frustration and anger, a parent may threaten to withdraw permanently from the life of the child in order to make the child conform. Sending a child to her or his room is a form of isolation and abandonment. It seems critically important to explain such action as a time for cooling off and thinking as opposed to punishment by isolation which can be interpreted as desertion. As children grow and develop, they soon learn that such threats of exclusion and desertion are also used by friends. This becomes particularly acute in the adolescent years when acceptance by the peer group is the sine qua non for one's sense of worth and value. Being shut out, banned, or ostracized from the group as a teenager for most is a fate worse than death. One becomes labeled as a loser, a loner, a nerd, or some other denigrating epithet and experiences either being set adrift alone on a sea of nothingness or the young person may become a scapegoat for the in-group. The group may transfer its own sense of shame to this individual and s/he becomes a cipher for everyone else's shame. In either case, the adolescent feels keenly the burning sting of rejection and experiences being deserted and abandoned. This fear of desertion and abandonment also carries over into adult life.

Controlling husbands may use desertion shame to coerce spouses into remaining in abusive situations. There is the threat of withdrawing economic and social support. Many women in abusive situations when asked why they did not leave indicated that the thought of being deserted and the shame of abandonment would be more than they could tolerate. They believed that intolerable shame would be experienced if family and friends knew that a separation or divorce was imminent. Sexist comments such as, "Why can't she keep her husband?" or "If she only tried harder she could make the marriage go" or "I wonder what she's doing to drive her husband away?" only exacerbate the shame. After twelve years of constant abuse, a woman finally left the marriage, but not without considerable anxiety. She was concerned that no one would believe her story, and fearful of the judgmental comments which would be made by family and friends in addition to her own sense of failure in the marriage and the fact that she may have to spend the rest of her life alone. Otto Will rightly points out that desertion shame is a powerful weapon.

> Shame can be, and often is, used as a weapon. "You ought to be ashamed" at best raises doubt about one's deeds and thoughts, and "Shame on you!" can be a form of enduring curse. To "shame" is a way of putting onus on another person and can easily become a form of cruelty, accompanied as noted earlier, by the threat of abandonment, desertion, loss, ostracism, and death. The statement, "I'd rather be dead than face such shame" is not uncommon, nor is its suggested act.[29]

Sometimes when people experience misfortune which may not even be of their own doing, family, friends, and others may consciously avoid coming into contact with them. It is as though misfortune is contagious or that association with someone who has experienced this kind of difficulty deserves to be punished. This feeling was expressed by a farmer who was being foreclosed upon through no real fault of his own. He was caught up in the economic machinations of a system which enveloped and strangled him. When others in the community heard about it, they began to avoid him and he became a social pariah. Being deserted by friends and acquaintances increased his sense of shame, though there was no ethical or moral culpability involved with this particular experience.

Desertion shame is a powerfully controlling force often exercised by those in authority who wish to break the pride or spirit of others. Such shaming tactics are used in the name of discipline whenever they are implemented. Control is exercised through the use of derogatory names, attacks on one's character, and the persistent belittling and demeaning of all the person is or does.

Another example of desertion shame is the brutal punishment designed for control purposes within the prison setting. Solitary confinement is the punishment reserved for those who do not conform. Human beings are by nature social creatures and to be forcefully removed from the social setting cuts to the very core of human need. Whether the desertion or abandonment is physical, psychological, social, or spiritual, the message is either that you are not worth enough to be concerned about or you will be shamed into conformity by the powers that be. Hence the person is deserted and abandoned, bereft of social interaction and left to wither on a vine which is not nourished with the flow of energy from other people.

Religious bodies have historically utilized the tactic of excommunication to discipline an individual or group. This action was implemented for a variety of offenses ranging from apostasy to refusal to conform to prevailing practices, pieties, or theological formulations. Invoking the ban of the community and in the action implicitly threatening the offending party with the abandonment of God was designed to elicit repentance. It is evidence of a powerful shaming tactic created to control others, but invoked for the good of the person or group labeled as nonconformist and therefore dangerous. Whether construed as punishment (solitary confinement) or discipline (excommunication), the common denominator is the shame of being deserted or abandoned by others.

The implications of desertion as disgrace shame could be pursued and illustrated in a variety of other ways. The reader may wish to examine her or his own life experience to discover the power of this dynamic. Once again, it is a human experience for which forgiveness does not seem to be the primary religious antidote. The shame dynamic requires another approach in order that the person might be liberated from its debilitating effects.

DISHONOR AS A SHAME DYNAMIC

Dishonor has to do with being stripped of a sense of dignity and integrity which results in horrible humiliation. Perhaps the most poignant example is that of defeat in battle whereby the vanquished experience dishonor in the face of defeat. The Scriptures cite several instances in which shame as dishonor is so experienced. A few such references are: II Chronicles 32:21, Nehemiah 1:3, Isaiah 22:17–18, Jeremiah 2:36, 9:19, 46:24, and 48:1. The shame and dishonor of defeat is so great in the mind of King Saul that rather than face the humiliation of capture and likely an ignominious death at the hands of his captors, he takes his own life (I Samuel 31), or as the narrative in II Samuel 1 recounts the situation, he persuades a passing Amalekite to slay him. History is replete with stories which depict the victors humiliating the vanquished with the shame of defeat. Land and people are pillaged and raped. Those who are taken prisoner are bound in chains, and deprived of dignity, decency, and all human rights. The past as well as the present bears witness to the reality of dishonor for nations who refuse to negotiate peace on any terms unless it is peace with honor.

Because the shame of dishonor is so excruciatingly painful, the corporate and individual prayers offered, particularly in the imprecatory psalms, are often for the humiliating defeat of the enemy. One of the more poignant expressions of this desire is written in Psalm 109:28-29.

Let them curse (the enemy), but do thou bless (the psalmist)!
Let my assailants be put to shame; may thy servant be glad!

May my accusers be clothed with dishonor; may they be
wrapped in their own shame as in a mantle!

A partial listing of additional passages includes: Psalm 25:2-3;
35:4,26; 40:14-15; 53:5; 57:3, 70:2-3; 71:13, 24; 78:66; 79:12,
83:16-17; 89:45; 119:78; 129:5 and 132:18. In each instance there is
either a corporate or individual prayer, wish, or hope which is
nurtured; namely, that the enemy experience the ignominy of defeat. It is bad enough to have to face oneself in the wake of such
defeat; it borders on the intolerable to have to face others. Nations,
tribes, families, and individuals cannot countenance defeat for it
means facing the ridicule of others as well as the self. A severe blow
to pride is struck in the experience of defeat. Donald Nathanson in
writing about shaming systems speaks of nations and individuals
existing on what he calls the shame/pride axis. He outlines the
manner in which this impacts individual and family behavior as
well as national image and politics.[30]
    The experience of defeat is occasioned by a variety of causes for
both groups and individuals. There may be prevailing circumstances which preclude the possibility of success or established
goals may be totally unrealistic. Lack of skill, knowledge, understanding, or ability may also spell defeat. Whatever the cause, a
sense of shame is elicited because defeat in our society is not tolerated and when it is exposed, the natural inclination is to want to hide
or, worse yet, to utterly despair. For the individual, defeat evokes
feelings of worthlessness and self-depreciation, prompting the person to once again want to hide because she or he has "lost face."
The experience of constant defeat in any competitive situation,
whether it be academics, athletics, or even human relationships, or
the inability to maintain something one already has such as property
and position all result in feelings of shame.
    If the defeat is publicly exposed, the sense of shame is propor-
tionately increased. People who are defeated often exhibit the same
in their body language. They hang their heads, hide their faces,
move with a stultifying gait, and wish to recede into the shadows
and away from the light where exposure may be experienced.
    The sense of dishonor as shame may take the shape of weakness,
whether that be physical, emotional, or spiritual in nature. Strength

has always been considered a necessary quality if one is to survive. "Whatever you do, don't let on that you are weak." "Keep your chin up!" "Be tough, be strong!" "Don't act like a sissy!" "Don't be a weakling!" The list of imperatives admonishing people not to be weak is infinite. This stoic disposition toward life refuses to acknowledge pleasure or pain, for seemingly any expression of passion or emotion is tantamount to admitting to the shame of weakness. It exposes the fear of vulnerability and the dread that the person is not in control of the situation.

This concern for weakness is noted in the arena of faith as well. When confronted with a catastrophic crisis, some Christians believe that any display of emotion is evidence of a weak faith. "If I had enough faith, I would be able to withstand this situation." "If my faith weren't so weak, I wouldn't let this bother me." These expressions of concern are indicative of the fact that one can easily experience shaming in the walk of faith. In a later chapter, consideration will be given to the role of faith in overcoming a debilitating sense of shame when properly understood. Suffice it to say at this point that the journey of faith can also be a shaming experience.

In keeping with one of the basic concerns of this book, it is well to point out once again that these shame feelings resulting from feelings of defeat or weakness more often than not do not call for a declaration of forgiveness for having violated a moral or ethical precept. Rather it is a description of human experience which can be paralyzing and debilitating which requires another paradigm from the faith tradition in order that people might hear the "good news."

DEFECTIVENESS AS A SHAME DYNAMIC

Another powerful dynamic of shame comes with a sense of feeling defective. This has a number of dimensions to it in terms of its being experienced as disgrace shame. Attention will be given to four specific aspects.

Physically Defective

Any kind of physical illness, anomaly, or disability may result in a person feeling "abnormal" or "different." A few examples from the biblical witness will illustrate the point. The phenomenon of infertility, for example, was an excruciatingly powerful source of pain for many women. The experience of Sarai (Genesis 16) indicates the incredible shame of not being able to bear children. Hannah (I Samuel 1:4-5) is an example of another who experienced the shame of a "closed womb," as it was often referred to in the ancient world (I Samuel 1:3-20). The curse of Elizabeth and Zechariah was that she was barren (Luke 1:7). That same shaming experience can be heard today when people question young married couples about their plans for a family.

In the ancient world, those who were captured in battle were often cruelly mutilated so as to make them physically defective. Judges 1:6-7 describes the removal of thumbs and the big toes from those who were conquered in battle to make them physically defective. The custom of castrating for males made them physically defective. The strange story of cutting off half a beard (II Samuel 10:4–5) was done in order to humiliate the victims and make them physically defective. The sense of defectiveness, for whatever the reason, evokes a sense of shame.

Birth defects which have disabled so many children were once treated with an immense amount of secrecy for the shame of having a child who was not normal. People who may be confined to a wheelchair, for example, whether because of accident, illness, or an anomaly from birth have often experienced a sense of shame for not being normal. The shame may be articulated as anger for being thus confined or may be expressed as despair because of the permanent nature of the condition. If one is maliciously labeled as a cripple, has had disparaging remarks made about one's condition, or is avoided because of a disability, the power of shame often comes to the fore. The person feels out of the mainstream of society and is treated accordingly. Fortunately, that social attitude is beginning to change and considerations for access for the physically disabled are slowly being implemented; nonetheless, the stigma still remains in many sectors of our society.

The loss or even impairment of one of the basic senses may evoke shame. The shame may be expressed in the form of denial in relationship to the loss or impairment. A friend of mine resolutely refused to accept the fact that his sense of hearing was virtually gone. The utilization of a hearing aid would be an admission that he was physically defective and might be labeled accordingly. I can remember the taunts of "four eyes" when I donned my first set of glasses my freshman year in high school. I was ashamed to wear them not only because it meant that my eyes were not perfect, but more so because I knew that the taunts and jeers of peers would be unmerciful. I would wear them only when absolutely necessary to avoid the shame associated with being set apart and teased for my defective eyesight.

A visible birthmark, scar, skin anomaly, or any other kind of deformity which may make a person self-conscious about her or his appearance may issue in a sense of shame about one's appearance.

Physical illness is also equated with physical defectiveness and hence shame. In the ancient world, lepers were relegated to isolated colonies not only for hygienic reasons, but because there was great shame in being a leper. The stigma was that it was a plague and as a result the person was impure. (Note Leviticus chapters 13 and 14 for the extensive regulations.)

Thus the experience of physical illness may be a source of shame for some people because illness is a deviation from the norm of health. Friends and parishioners of mine have asked me to keep their illness confidential because they did not want others to know they were ill. Parishioners have asked that their names *not* be mentioned in the general prayer of the church for healing. This may be evidence of discretionary shame, whereby the person wishes to keep private the illness so that boundaries are not transgressed. But often it is an expression of disgrace shame and the person refuses to acknowledge that s/he is even ill and therefore out of control of the situation.

If there is any alteration in physical appearance, as sometimes happens with cancer patients, for example, a sense of shame may be evoked and the person will desire to remain hidden from others. If the patient feels that others may see her or him as being repulsive because of the bodily changes that have occurred, she/he may prefer the safety of isolation, rather than the exposure and possible shame feelings which may ensue. From another perspective, family or friends may refuse to see a person who is very ill and who has suffered the ravages of a terminal illness. It may remind them of their own mortality, but it is also the expression of shame in being associated with another person who is no longer healthy.

The aging process can also bring with it its own sense of shame, particularly as time begins to exact a physical toll on people. The lament is often heard about not being able to do what once was possible. The appearance of other aging signs such as increased impairment in the basic senses or lack of mobility bring people face to face with physical limitations which preclude certain personal expectations. For some in a society where youth is idolized and aging is a demeaning experience, shame about one's physical situation may be hidden under a cloak of depression. The sense of shame for one's physical being may reach its epitome when people become incontinent and/or are forced to rely exclusively upon others for their every need.

The current concern which centers on body image in our society and our sense of physicality can also occasion a deep sense of shame. Eating disorders such as anorexia nervosa and bulimia may be associated with obsessive-compulsive behavior as it relates to body image. "I am ashamed of the way I look" or "I am ashamed of how fat I am" are common expressions articulated by young and old of both genders in our society. The idealization of a desirable figure and physique has become a multibillion-dollar business. Fundamental to most advertisements in this arena is the shame of not having a perfect body, however that might be imaged. Marketers create dissatisfaction by holding up the mythical "10" as an image to which all should aspire if they are to expect acceptance.

Obviously this obsession with bodily shape is directly related to sexuality. An image of the perfect female or male sexual partner is directly linked to body size, proportion, and development. How many relationships have never had the opportunity to develop because this mythical idol of the perfect body has become a barrier? Whereas physical attributes may be played down by most of us and we say that "beauty is only skin deep," nonetheless, in our subconscious, we tend to make evaluative judgments about others and ourselves based on the idealized or idolized images which have been created. Most of us find ourselves falling woefully short of the ideal and develop a concomitant sense of shame as a result. Donald Nathanson devotes a chapter, entitled "Size and Shape," to the discussion surrounding body image. Tall is better than short, thin is better than plump. He says,

> There is an infinitude of possible patterns that can be made into reasons for pride or shame. If the possession of an attribute can make us proud, the sudden "loss" of that possession will cause shame, no matter what the nature of the attribute.[31]

In a male-dominated and patriarchal society, undergirded by the sexist presuppositions and assumptions of such a system, shame can be associated with gender. As was previously noted, Anne Wilson Schaef writes about the "original sin of being born female."[32] Overtly and covertly we have operated with the gender-specific images passed down to us by society and the church. The designation of women as inferior may have been fostered by Freud, but it has deep roots in our social as well as our ecclesiastical history.[33] Being female is more than being "deficient"–it is being physically "defective." Thus for centuries women have been shamed for being women and have received messages concerning their unacceptability because of their gender.

Sexual orientation historically has also had an immense amount of shame associated with it. Once again, those who are labeled as different are judged accordingly. Not only the individual, but the family as well, is castigated and condemned. Lesbians and gays often experience not only the shame from being labeled physically defective, but also suffer the shame of desertion and abandonment by others. The current AIDS epidemic has compounded the grief process for victims and their families because the stigma of shame fostered by church and society has designated these people as social pariahs. Homophobia is a rampant phenomenon in our society. Discrimination, injustice, and violence are perpetrated without compunction or guilt because the sexual orientation of some people is different from the norm. The metaphor utilized by homosexuals as they claim their sexual identity is that they have "come out of the closet." This is indicative of the shame they felt for the way in which they have been created.

The whole issue of racism might also be lodged in this category of being physically defective. In a society basically governed by Caucasians, with Caucasian norms, images, values, and ideas, people of color may be shamed because they are not white. Discrimination runs wide and deep in our society in both overt and covert forms. It is one of the conundrums of an allegedly civilized and sophisticated society that people are still judged on the basis of skin pigmentation. Social as well as religious arguments have been marshaled over the centuries to justify this inexcusable discriminatory attitude, and the shame for not being white is a significant part of this scenario.

My friends who are people of color often speak about the phenomenon of invisibility. If one is not a part of the dominant culture and race, one is often discounted and disregarded. There are repeated incidences of waiting in a restaurant to be served or at a cash register to pay for an item where the person is ignored, treated as being invisible. My friends have stated that they not only feel physically defective, they feel physically invisible!

This list of examples is obviously not exhaustive. Each reader can likely add her or his own experiences of shame associated with feeling physically defective. As we come to understand the powerful influence of shame from being physically defective in our own lives, our consciousness is raised concerning the multiplicity of ways in which, through our own prejudices and biases, we have perpetuated or used shame in relationship to others.

Enormous amounts of time, money, and energy are invested in attempting to hide any kind of actual or perceived physical defectiveness, in order to escape the sense of shame which may accompany that experience.

Emotionally Defective

One of the ways in which the Scriptures appear to describe the phenomenon of mental illness is to place it in the category of demon possession. The heart-rending narrative of the Gerasene demonic in Mark 5 is a good example. His emotional illness obviously manifested itself in violence to others as well as to himself. He was isolated from the mainstream of society and feared by those who had no explanation for such a phenomenon except to attribute it to demons.

Today people may also experience shame if they perceive themselves or are believed to be emotionally defective. Anyone who is born with or who develops any kind of emotional or mental illness may experience the shame of being "different," "unusual," or "pitiful" for his or her condition.

There was a time in our society when children who were born with or developed any kind of emotional difficulties were quietly sequestered at home or spirited away to some institution. The family experienced a sense of shame for having a "defective child," one who was not normal and who therefore was the source of a great deal of embarrassment. We see once again the need for hiding and secrecy lest exposure result in anticipated or imagined social rejection.

The shame stigma is experienced by anyone whose emotional circuits cannot withstand the pressures occasioned by the exigencies of life. We euphemistically refer to people as having "nervous breakdowns" or a "mental collapse," or as being "emotionally unstable." Whereas for the most part disease of the body is acceptable, an illness which affects the mind precipitates an immense amount of fear. The fear is expressed by the uninformed in the terminology which is often used to describe people with mental illness or emotional problems. They are said to be "crazy," "nuts," "whacko," "odd," "peculiar," "strange," "bonkers," or a variety of other denigrating designations. They are not only labeled as different and defective, but in fact are set apart and many times ostracized and institutionalized out of sight from the rest of society.

Implicit in the judgment is that such people are abnormal and are incapable of "taking it"! I wonder how many people have avoided seeking help for emotional problems because of the stigma associated with receiving therapy. One of the more notable examples of this came in the 1972 presidential campaign in which the vice-presidential nominee on the Democratic ticket was literally forced to relinquish that position because he had received assistance for his emotional problems. Shame stems often out of social ignorance concerning emotional or mental situations.

Utilizing the cancer metaphor, the shame metastasizes within the family system. The malignancy permeates the entire family system, so that in some instances family members will disassociate themselves from the person in the family who is experiencing these problems. We don't want to be associated with anyone who is crazy nor admit or claim them as a part of the family. The fear seems to be that the emotional problems may be contagious or that family members will be contaminated by this "bad apple" in the barrel. The conspiracy of silence prevails.

As a parish pastor, I remember the guardedness with which families spoke when a family member was receiving psychiatric treatment. No one wanted to admit that a relative had been admitted to the "psych ward." In addition to the epithets noted earlier, I can remember people in the community referring to the psychiatric ward as the "funny farm," "looney bin," or the "nut house." People who received treatment and were released were often treated with suspicion, avoided, or mocked, thus increasing the already existing sense of shame.

Some people are ridiculed because they "feel too much"! They draw remarks such as, "you are just too sensitive." "Why don't you lighten up on the feelings?" As a person who teaches in pastoral care, I have often experienced sarcastic remarks such as, "You are one of those 'touchy-feely' types." "Why aren't you involved in a 'real' theological discipline?" The insinuation is that if one deals with the affective dimension of life, it is of less value than work in the cognitive arena. Any rejoinder to that kind of shaming usually draws further derision. "See, I told you so; you pastoral-care types are all alike." The shame is compounded by a gross generalization that shames one even further.

The other end of the spectrum is that some people are shamed because they feel too little. As with the person who feels too much, the person who feels too little may have been socialized in such a way that she or he was told that feelings are bad. Feelings are to be kept under control, ignored, or repressed. Such people are often accused of being cold and calculating, with "ice water in their veins." In both instances–feeling either too much or too little–the person is shamed by others and finally internalizes the messages to the point of shaming the self for being who she/he is.

Another powerful experience of shame happens to those of us who have experienced a suicide in our family. We know about the intensity of the shame and the fear of being labeled as emotionally defective by association. In suicide survivors groups in which I have participated, one of the topics of discussion often centered around our reticence even to talk about the event. In processing my own grief through the tragedy and trauma, I came to the conclusion that my own shame was a concern that my whole family would be labeled as mentally or emotionally defective. Social, but especially ecclesiastical, judgmentalism exacerbates the anguish and agony of such an emotionally wrenching experience. In some churches the custom still prevails that the body of someone who has completed suicide shall not be brought into the sanctuary. There were prohibitions against the body being buried within the confines of the cemetery. Judgments were made about the eternal disposition of the soul of the suicide victim, who had committed the unforgivable sin. Family members, who have been termed "suicide survivors," have experienced ostracism and the pain of public humiliation and ridicule. Every such experience, whether intentional or inadvertent, serves to increase the painful sense of shame. Thus, one not only has grief to deal with, but the shame as well.

Socially Defective

The religious prohibitions which Jesus violated often had to do with his social relationships. "Why does your teacher eat with tax collectors and sinners?" (Matthew 9:11 and parallels). Decent and self-respecting people do not associate with such; it is shameful behavior to do so. The irony of the parable of the Good Samaritan (Luke 15:11-32), which Jesus uses as an explanation for his association with those who were not socially acceptable, is that the person who understood the command to be a neighbor was a Samaritan, a social outcast in Jesus' day. Jesus' delineation in his parable of the judgment in Matthew 25 are all examples of those who might be considered as social outcasts for economic or political reasons. Those who are hungry, thirsty, strangers, unclothed, sick, and imprisoned are not the normal run-of-the-mill folks. They are socially ostracized, abnormal, and in that sense socially defective.

There seems to be an intrinsic need to find scapegoats for the frustrations, disappointments, and ills of society. Characteristically, we as human beings have designated individuals or groups to function in that capacity. We tend to assign that role to those we deem as different or unacceptable. This process often begins very early in life as children begin to experience social grouping. Whatever the criteria for inclusion in a group may be, and however those criteria are formulated, the group soon makes a determination of who is "in" and who is "out." This decision may be based on any number of factors from youngster's physical attributes, emotional demeanor, racial or ethnic background, social or economic condition, or personality, to whether s/he just happened to be in the wrong place at the right time. This child is assigned the role of the scapegoat and is labeled with a variety of names by the other children. The child soon takes on that shame identity as one who does not fit, and is not accepted or included. Even if there is no apparent reason, the child may be designated as "it" and absorb all of the taunts, teasing, jeers, mockery, shame, and venom of the whole group.

As children mature into adolescents, the importance of being accepted by a group takes on even greater significance. Unless there is some kind of substantive change or someone else is assigned the role of scapegoat, the label in adolescence carries over from childhood. The pain of the shame is increased with the greater social awareness of the maturing adolescent. As I recall, I often spent time alone, fantasizing about what might be someday, desperately trying to please others in order to gain their friendship or feeling resigned to suffer the plight of my own fate. In that sense, the adolescent years were among the most painful, and I suspect that is true for many young people who do not "fit" or who feel like social misfits. One becomes ashamed of oneself, believing that one is socially defective. As Erik Erikson points out, the development of identity is the critical task of the adolescent years,[34] and shame-based identities are often the result because the adolescent feels socially defective. It is important to note once again that this feeling arises not because of some moral or ethical issue, but rather is intricately involved with one's developing self-concept. It has to do with "being" and not principally with "doing."

It is no mystery that, having learned the "in" and "out" group designation in childhood and adolescence, the same dynamics carry over into adult life. For example, people who are single have often shared the feeling that somehow they are socially defective because they are not married. The prevailing social norms and values dictate that one is incomplete or defective socially if one is not married. Activities in society in general and in the church specifically are often geared for couples and/or families. Whether by choice, chance, or circumstance, a person remaining single is often the occasion for speculation on the part of other people. "Why doesn't she get married?" "What's the matter with him; why can't he find a partner?" The inference and insinuation is that there must be something wrong with these folks; they are socially defective and hence often treated as social misfits.

The same message may be sent to those who are individually or as a group economically deprived. I vividly remember the feeling of shame for not having the latest style in clothing. Even though I came from a very loving home, once I began school, it became immediately evident to me that I did not come from the most affluent family in the neighborhood. Teasing and taunting about how one dresses can cut deeply into the psyche of a schoolchild. As a family we were not poverty-stricken, but we did not have the financial wherewithal to keep up with the more affluent. Insidiously, the social message gets communicated and picked up that you should be ashamed of yourself. "How can you appear in public so shabbily dressed? Shame on you!" Even though those precise words likely were never spoken, the feeling remains as a vivid memory. I can painfully remember thinking, "Who would ever want me as a friend, much less a spouse!" It is important to remember that there is a distinction between reality and perception. The person may perceive that she/he is thus regarded, and the fact may be that the perception is distorted. Nonetheless, there is often substance to the perception. I can recall many days remaining indoors during the free period, reading and writing rather than facing the jeers and taunts of my peers.

Having considered my own relatively limited experience with shame socially and economically, it is virtually inconceivable to me what that must feel like when it is a permanent condition. Whatever the reason or circumstances, being numbered among the poor in our nation becomes a shame issue. The messages which are explicitly or implicitly sent to the underprivileged is that they are "lazy," "dumb," "irresponsible," "leeches," or a plethora of other demeaning designations. Labels are sticky and once having been applied to a person or group of persons, a label is difficult to remove.

It is my contention that one of the ways of dealing with shame, as will be more explicitly delineated in the next chapter, is to attempt to shift it to others. Perhaps this is why each society feels as if it needs people who can be labeled as "social misfits" who bear the resentments and recriminations of the whole society. Often such people are relegated to institutions which retain them as sociopaths, psychopaths, or incorrigibles. While it is self-evident that there are people who are a danger to others as well as themselves, I wonder about the genesis of such behavior and self-understanding. I am speculating that shame had a strong role in defining who they were as persons. I have not had extensive experience in ministry related to those so labeled, except in the field of alcohol and drug abuse. I can attest to the fact that the shame issue is a decisive factor at work in addiction. As Fossum and Mason have so concretely demonstrated, the shame issue is a dynamic operative both in those who are afflicted and those who are affected by addiction.[35]

Spiritually Defective

"Now concerning spiritual gifts, people of God, I do not want you to be uninformed" (I Corinthians 12:1). With this statement, the Apostle Paul introduces three chapters in this epistle (12-14) concerning the nature and use of the so-called spiritual gifts. There were those who made claim to greater authority and importance because they possessed what they felt were superior gifts. The situation lends itself to a strong shaming possibility, not only in the pride some may have in the gift which they have been given, but in holding up the gift in order to shame others who do not have that gift, and hence are considered to be defective.

The sense of shame may arise if one feels defective in the expression of one's own personal piety. I must confess to being green with envy at the alleged completeness and sanctity in the lives of some of the saints. I suspect that others have the same feeling, as we for the most part put ourselves to shame because our spiritual life is in shambles. If I felt guilty about it, perhaps I would be prompted to rectify or at least address the situation. But more often than not, I wrestle not with guilt, but with shame. The messages run like this, "You are a worthless person, pastor, professor because your prayer life is not disciplined." "Shame on you, how can you presume to teach and/or preach to others when you don't have your act together?" The admonishment in our rite of ordination charges us to be models of godly life and conversation in our ministry. The waves of shame envelop to the point of drowning. "You are a worthless person!" Like the well-intentioned addict, one vows to do better, to be more disciplined and more intentional, and one is set up for even more shame–the shame of failure and the shame of concluding that one is spiritually defective.

The sense of shame for being spiritually defective may arise if one does not meet the expectations of others with regard to doctrinal issues. A given belief system is established as being normative and any deviation from that system brings sharp invectives and judgmental condemnation. It is always of interest to me to read Letters to the Editor in religious publications and other such columns wherein personal opinions are given free expression. More often than not, opinions are not expressed, but the column becomes a forum for fiery attacks on others who "do not believe as I do!" The presumption of truth assumed by the writer issues in sharp polemical attacks on the arrogance of assuming such a position. Rarely does the writer acknowledge other would-be adversaries who are not in agreement– would-be adversaries whose existence belies arrogance. Implicit is the shaming of those who would allegedly pervert the essence of the faith by their misguided thinking and belief system. The necessity for being right may in and of itself betray a shame-based person, but to privately or publicly call the "non-believer" or "heretic" to task is tantamount to being a defender of the faith. I have participated in a number of conversations about theological issues where the dialogue turned into a diatribe or where the discussion deteriorated into a personal exchange of demeaning and degrading epithets. All issued, of course, in the name of purity and truth. Theological formulations can be transformed into sham intellectual idols and defended by shaming those who might dare to call them into question. In some quarters hierarchical authority may be invoked and the threat of exclusion by excommunication for failure to conform constitutes a threat that carries great power.

The shame of being spiritually defective may find expression also in the very nature of religious experience. Once again it is the authoritative declaration of what is considered normative by which the judgment is made. The assumption seems to be that my personal religious experience is the only valid one. Shame on you if yours does not conform to mine, as it is obviously inauthentic and invalid. The Apostle Paul in particular addresses this issue in his First Letter to the Church at Corinth. (Note I Corinthians 3 in particular.) Factionalism, personality cults, and decisiveness based on religious experience have no place within the faith community. The religious experience of varying people and groups is different. There is room for diversity of experiences. As a matter of fact, it can add to the richness of the community unless a person or group within the community requires conformity or uniformity of experience. The tactic employed to coerce conformity more often than not is shame. It is evident that once again the "in" versus the "out" group mentality is employed.

Being judged or labeled as defective by others or the self, whether it involves the physical, emotional, social, or spiritual realm, touches the lives of most if not all people. In most instances, moral and ethical considerations are nonexistent or at best minimal, so the dynamic operative is not that of guilt, but of shame. In each instance, the person judges her or himself–or is judged by others–as being defective, and may suffer an insufferable experience of disgrace shame. When the shame message that one is defective is given frequently enough, the person soon views her or himself in that manner and assumes the shame identity, responding and living accordingly in relationship to God, others, and the self.

DEFILEMENT AS A SHAME DYNAMIC

The biblical paradigm for this experience is the II Samuel 13 narrative of Tamar and Amnon. Much might be said about the intrafamilial dynamics of the whole situation within the Davidic household, but what catches my attention is the shame reaction on the part of both the victim and the perpetrator. The scenario, with all of its lustful deceit, is established in verses 1-6, with King David's unknowing complicity noted in verse seven. With his skillful scheming, Amnon finally succeeds in getting his half-sister alone with him in his chamber. His sexual invitation is refused by Tamar, who responds to his suggestion by saying, "No, my brother, do not force me; for such a thing is not done in Israel; do not do this wanton folly. As for me, where could I carry my shame? And as for you,

you would be as one of the wanton fools in Israel" (II Samuel 13:13). Tamar rightfully names the shame as the issue for her. Since this is a situation involving force, Tamar would not incur guilt for complicity, but rather shame for being compromised against her will. She attempts to appeal to his reason, citing the fact that the king would in all likelihood grant permission for Amnon to have her (verse 13), but he is not willing to do that and rapes her.

Amnon's response to the incident is hatred and anger. He was guilty of rape and rather than acknowledging his guilt, he reacts with rage, which is often a shame defense. He forcefully banishes Tamar from his presence so that he is not reminded either of his guilt for his violent act or his shame as the perpetrator. Her shame response is poignantly recorded in II Samuel 13:19, "And Tamar put ashes on her head, and rent the long robe which she wore; and she laid her hand on her head, and went away, crying aloud as she went." In verse 20b her plight is further noted, "So Tamar dwelt, a desolate woman in her brother Absalom's house." Her shame is centered in her being violently raped and her concomitant sense of defilement. The social impact of now being considered as damaged property is monumental. The Scriptures give us no further details concerning her life subsequent to the rape. The rest of the story and the familial implications for David, Amnon, and Absalom are detailed in the rest of chapter thirteen.

It should also be noted that males as well as females are sexually abused and suffer the consequences of disgrace shame. The number of cases is increasing in which it has been determined that a young boy has been sexually abused by another. As with their female counterparts, the traumatic nature of the experience often is buried deeply within the psyche so as to avoid the pain of memory. Adult males who are sexually violated experience a tremendous amount of shame. They often feel as if they should have been able to avoid or stop the experience. The experience is appropriated not only as a physical attack upon their person, but also as a demeaning of their identity as males.

This final category is one laden with an immense amount of emotional trauma. The shame which comes about through defilement or invasiveness often leaves the person feeling dirty, demeaned, despoiled, and desecrated. Those who have experienced the traumatic violence of sexual abuse often experience the shame of defilement. Females in a sexist society experience the added burden of being labeled or thought of as damaged property. The mystique around the state of virginity and all which that symbolizes for males and females irrespective of the circumstance plays a powerful role. In this realm of experience it is particularly important to make the distinction between guilt and shame. Victims have often shared what they termed guilt for the incident. Guilt would give the inference that the victim is somehow responsible or to be blamed for what occurred and stands in need of forgiveness for the act. Rape and incest victims are *not responsible* for what happens to them, yet they have strong feelings which may be best described as defilement, with the result that they feel dirty and in need of cleansing.

Rape by definition is a violent violation of a person's body, mind, and spirit. Incest is also an invasive violation of another person by a perpetrator who is a member of one's own family. The reaction may vary with the circumstances and the individuals involved, but in many situations the sense of defilement is so strong that the person may deny what has happened, disown her or his own history, disassociate emotionally, and despair spiritually. There is reticence for a variety of reasons to embrace the reality of what has happened. When these persons begin to deal with the trauma, many express this sense of defilement. This episode from the biblical witness may illustrate the dynamics as well as any.

Marie Fortune has pointed out that in the biblical narrative concerning the rape of Dinah (Genesis 34), the critical issue is not so much the violence against the person as it is concern for protecting the male rights over women in the ancient society.[36] I would concur completely with that analysis, but would also state that even that consideration does not obviate the shame experienced by those who were violated. Nothing could restore the personal sense of worth and value that was lost. Disgrace shame would dominate her life because the boundaries of discretionary shame were not heeded.

Many women and men carry not only the physical, but the emotional and spiritual scars of shame occasioned by defilement which leaves them feeling despoiled, demeaned, and has often been expressed to me a sense of being "dirty." The invasive nature of incest and rape results in a sense of being dirty and a compelling sense of needing to be cleansed. The societal attitudes and dispositions often blame the victim, which only exacerbates the sense of shame. Thus, the painful experience may be repressed out of conscious awareness because it is so overwhelming, but the resultant shame is still evident in that person's life. It may take the form of low self-esteem, denigrating self-evaluation, a despairing sense of worthlessness, or a proclivity to self-destruction. Susan Miller has pointed out that it is particularly in dealing with issues pertaining to sexuality that the interrelatedness of guilt and shame are experienced, and this often makes the distinction between the two difficult. In writing about the rape victim's shame she says, "the degradation inherent in the environment is experienced as so great that shame by mere association prevails, despite reason's counsel that the individual was not there by choice." In a relevant footnote she further explains that, "The painful emotion commonly described as survivor guilt probably includes a large component of (moral) shame. As an added complication, it is possible that guilt promotes shame as a punishment felt to be appropriate for actions perceived to be morally wrong."[37] In the chaos and confusion, care must be taken to assist the victim in clearly understanding the dynamics of this traumatic experience.

In terms of the spiritual dimension, the victim's sense of defilement shame occasioned by rape or incest does not call for confession, absolution, and forgiveness for this specific experience. *The victim is not* responsible or guilty for what has occurred. If the guilt-forgiveness paradigm is exercised, the person's sense of shame is likely to be increased. A different theological and pastoral paradigm needs to be developed in order to deal with shame.

As has been documented, shame manifests itself in feeling disgust with the self, a sense of deficiency, desertion, dishonor, defectiveness, or defilement. It is a powerfully pervasive phenomenon which touches the lives of all people even though it is often socially, culturally, religiously, and gender-specific in nature. Its power is so great that one can hardly dwell on the subject for any period of time before the focus must be shifted. The threat created by shame is so powerful and the feelings so poignant that elaborate defense mechanisms are created in order to survive. Consideration will be given to these defense strategies in the next chapter.

NOTES

1. Fossum, Merle and Marilyn Mason. *Facing Shame: Families in Recovery.* New York: W. W. Norton, 1986, p. 5.

2. Schneider, Carl D. *Shame, Exposure and Privacy.* Boston: Beacon Press, 1977, p. 22.

3. Bradshaw, John. *Healing the Shame that Binds You.* Deerfield Beech, FL: Health Communications Inc., 1988, p. 10.

4. Kaufman, Gershen. *Shame: The Power of Caring.* Cambridge: Schenkman Publishing Co., 1980, p. 9.

5. Kaufman, pp. 3-35.

6. Erikson, Erik. *Childhood and Society.* New York: W.W. Norton and Co., 1963 (2nd ed.), pp. 251-252.

7. Kaufman, pp. 37-79.

8. Mead, George Herbert. *Mind, Self, and Society.* Chicago: Chicago University Press, 1934.

9. Wurmser, Leon. *The Mask of Shame.* Baltimore: John Hopkins University Press, 1981.

10. Miller, Susan. *The Shame Experience.* Hillsdale, NJ: The Analytic Press, 1985, p. 9.

11. Miller, Susan. pp. 9-20.

12. Nathanson, Donald L. *The Many Faces of Shame.* New York: Guilford Press, 1987, p. 8.

13. Kinston, Warren. "The Shame of Narcissism." In Donald L. Nathanson (ed.), *The Many Faces of Shame.* New York: Guilford Press, 1987, p. 232.

14. Schneider, Carl D. "A Matured Sense of Shame." In Donald L. Nathanson (ed.), *The Many Faces of Shame.* New York: Guilford Press, 1987, p. 199.

15. Nathanson, p. 252.

16. Nathanson, p. 265.

17. Horney, Karen. *Our Inner Conflicts.* New York: W.W. Norton and Co., 1945.

18. Wurmer, Leon. "Shame: The Veiled Companion of Narcissism." In Donald L. Nathanson (ed), *The Many Faces of Shame.* New York: Guilford Press, 1987, p. 76.

19. Miller, Susan, p. 30.

20. Miller, William. *Why Christians Break Down.* Minneapolis: Augsburg Publishing House, 1973.

21. Adler, Alfred. *The Individual Psychology of Alfred Adler: A Systematic Presentation in Selections from His Writings.* (Edited by H. L. and R. R. Ansbacher). New York: Harper, 1956.

22. Nathanson, p. 258.

23. Kaufman, p. 27.

24. Schaef, Anne Wilson. *Woman's Reality.* Minneapolis: Winston Press, 1981, pp. 23-46.

25. Berke, Joseph H. "Shame and Envy." In Donald L. Nathanson (ed.), *The Many Faces of Shame*. New York: Guilford Press, 1987, p. 318-334.

26. Miller, Susan, p. 20.

27. Rank, Otto. *The Trauma of Birth*. New York: R. Brunner, 1952.

28. Nathanson, p. 252.

29. Will, Otto Allen, Jr. "The Sense of Shame in Psychosis: Random Comments on Shame in the Psychotic Experience." In Donald L. Nathanson (ed.), *The Many Faces of Shame*. New York: Guilford Press, 1987, p. 312.

30. Nathanson, pp. 246-269.

31. Nathanson, Donald. *Shame and Pride: Affect, Sex, and the Birth of the Self*. New York: W.W. Norton, 1992, p. 165.

32. Schaef, pp. 23-52

33. Bussert, Joy. *Battered Women*. Philadelphia: Division for Mission in North America-Lutheran Church in America, 1986.

34. Erikson, pp. 261-263.

35. Fossum and Mason, pp. 3-104.

36. Fortune, Marie. Lecture presented at Luther Northwestern Theological Seminary on January 26, 1990. See also: Brown, Joanne Carlson and Carole R. Bohn (eds.). *Christianity, Patriarchy, and Abuse*. New York: The Pilgrim Press, 1989.

37. Miller, Susan, p. 142.

Chapter Four

Defending Against Shame

The power of disgrace shame produces an intolerable degree of discomfort in the individual, or in an identified group for that matter. It is not possible to just "let it be." It must be defended against if one is to have any modicum of dignity. Oftentimes nearly all of a person's energy is channeled into the defense process in a kind of myopic fixation to obviate the shame, precluding creative and imaginative expression of one's self.

Gershen Kaufman indicates that there is no degree of predictability about the way in which an individual learns to defend her or himself against shame or any other emotion. Much is contingent once again upon the culture, context, and conditioning which the individual experiences in the social matrix of the family and other significant relationships. In addition to these external forces, Kaufman suggests that there is also the whole issue of temperament or the personality of each person which comes into play.[1] As the maturation and growth process proceeds in each person, the mechanisms which are selected are based on past experience and refined accordingly. Because of the potent power of shame, the defense mechanisms are utilized as a strategy for survival or as Kaufman terms them, an "adaptation" process in dealing with reality.[2] Defenses are necessary for human beings to exist, but it can happen that they are used only reactively rather than proactively. A helpful distinction between the modalities of defense is stated thus,

> Particularly following internalization, that psychological event which makes shame so intolerable, the self begins to develop strategies of defense against experiencing shame and strategies for the interpersonal transfer of experienced shame. To-

gether these dual modes comprise a general process of defense which encompasses both protecting against shame and dealing with it once shame has become activated. Strategies of DE-FENSE are essentially forward looking; they aim at protecting the self against further exposure and further experiences of shame. Strategies of TRANSFER, in contrast, are aroused only after some shame has begun to be felt.[3]

In surveying the variety of defense mechanisms used, they are as numerous as there are people, and they are nuanced accordingly with refined personal precision. Rather than making an attempt to enumerate all of them, I would like to focus on those which I have found to be most utilized by members of the faith community.

PERFECTIONISM

This defense seems to lead the parade, often developing out of a particular perspective on piety. The drive for perfection has nothing to do with the ability to morally or ethically distinguish between right and wrong. Rather it is a mercilessly demanding drive within the self which requires that the person perform as divine rather than human. The perfectionist cannot tolerate the frailties and foibles associated with being human. When the work or performance is less than perfect, less than that demanded by the idealized image of the self, the result is disgust with the self. (Refer to the first section in the previous chapter.)

I concur with Kaufman when he indicates that this defense mechanism is developed early in life, often as a result of unreasonable parental expectations. He says, "Whenever parental love, acceptance, or pride become dependent upon a child's performance in the world, the seeds of perfectionism are being sown."[4]

The person with a shame-based identity reasons that one of the ways to avoid the painful experience of shame is to live perfectly or flawlessly, thus theoretically eliminating any possibility for criticism or attack which would elicit shame. Perfection may be a divine attribute, but it is an impossible human attainment. The failure to achieve perfection does not result in the individual abandoning the project; rather the person exerts even greater effort to achieve this impossible goal. A vicious circle of effort, failure, renewed effort, and then greater failure is set in motion. The person has charted a course on a downward spiral which culminates in frustration and exhaustion. The best is never good enough!

The curse of perfectionism is a two-edged sword. It may be an externally imposed standard wherein the child receives the message that acceptability is predicated on the basis of performance, whether that be in the arena of behavior or, later, in achievements in various realms of endeavor such as academics, drama, sports, or leadership. Often this external demand for perfection on the part of parents and significant others is actually an effort at compensating for their own sense of shame by vicariously living out their needs in the lives of their children.

Acceptability is externally referented. Therefore the worth and value of a person is always dependent upon what others say. In the parlance of chemical dependency language, the person learns to be "codependent."[5] People who are codependent more often than not are shame-based people. The codependence may be an attempt to compensate for the shame of having a family member or significant other who is labeled as being chemically dependent. The genesis of the need to protect the user from the consequences of her or his use may be attributed to the need to hide the reality from the outside world. The phenomenon of denial is the behavioral result, but the reason for the denial may be attributed in large part to the disgrace shame which people who are close to the chemically dependent person experience.

The other edge of the sword is the internal demand for perfection which the person develops as a result of the external messages. It is no longer another person who is making the demands; rather the person makes the demand of perfection upon her or himself since s/he is convinced that acceptability and lovability are at stake. It is an attempt to make up for perceived deficiencies in the self or others. When the person fails, the demand for perfection can be projected on to someone else and the never ending cycle perpetuates itself.

Vicious competitiveness can arise out of perfectionism when life's motto is "winning is not everything; it's the only thing!!" Envy rears its ugly head if others get ahead or excel. There is no celebration or joy in the accomplishments and success of others, for their achievements symbolize superiority as contrasted with the perfectionist's perceived sense of inferiority. Human relationships suffer immensely in the process.[6] Rather than suffering with those who suffer and rejoicing with those who are honored (I Corinthians 12:26), exactly the opposite occurs.

Human limitations are not tolerated because divine perfection is mandated. Even though members of the faith community have heard the proclamation of the "good news" that salvation does not come by perfect adherence to the law of God or external and internal human rules, this seems to be little more than an intellectual formulation. Affectively the person is compulsively driven by the demand for perfection in order to presumably earn acceptability with God, others, and the self. The perfectionist lives with the curse of being human with all of its imperfections. Despite this reality, the person attempts to live as though perfection were attainable and with this attitude is condemned to perpetual frustration. The Pauline insight is right on target, "For all who rely on works of the law are under a curse; for it is written, 'Cursed be every one who does not abide by all things written in the book of the law to do them'" (Galatians 3:10). It is easy to understand that if the demand for perfection is a powerful driving force in order to avoid the biting sting of shame and to earn acceptability on the human level, the same will be true in that person's relationship with God. The understanding and experience of God is predicated on the perceptions one develops in relationship to human beings.

Inevitably someone will insist that believers are mandated by Scripture to be perfect. After all, Jesus Himself said in the Sermon on the Mount, "You, therefore, must be perfect, as your heavenly Father is perfect" (Matthew 5:48). The Greek word used in this text does not refer to perfection as popularly understood, that is, being without sin, fault, error, or blemish. The injunction to "be perfect" is not an imperative to be interpreted negatively as asking for the impossible; rather it is an encouragement toward wholeness and growth in relationships. The Scripture also makes quite clear that those who would profess to be perfect or sinless are deceiving and lying to themselves (I John 1:8). The sanctification of life does not consist of a striving for perfection so that we can present ourselves as acceptable before

God. It is an exercise in growing in grace and in knowledge of a creative and loving God (Ephesians 4:15, II Peter 3:18).

SELF-RIGHTEOUSNESS

If one does not measure up in terms of perfectionism, another ploy in dealing with shame is to put others down. In the church this most often comes to expression as the so-called "holier than thou" attitude which is in effect self-righteousness. Since this is a negative term, it is rarely an epithet which any of us would lay claim to or admit about ourselves, yet it runs rampant in our relationships.

It is evident in the pervasive use of judgmentalism. Kaufman speaks of judgmentalism in conjunction with contempt. He says, "In the development of contempt as a characterological defending style, we have the seeds of a judgmental, fault finding, or condescending attitude in later human relationships."[7] Putting others down by labeling them as evil, bad, sinful, dangerous, nonbelievers, fanatics, radicals, liberals, conservatives, or some other pejorative term, serves in the accuser's mind as establishing her or him as superior. Rather than deal with one's own sense of shame, the shame is projected onto others. The rationale seems to be that if I can put others down, I will feel better about myself. The biblical paradigm for this attitude is noted in Luke 18:9-14 in Jesus' parable of the Pharisee and the publican. "God I thank thee that I am not like other people." The attitude comes off as being arrogant, but often beneath the veneer of haughtiness, smugness, and self-righteousness is a person who cannot come to terms with her or his own sense of shame. "The contradiction between an 'inflated' self-concept and a self that needs reassurance of its worth becomes less 'curious' if we assume that what is being described is the operation of shame."[8]

Self-righteousness as a defense carries within it the seeds of judgmentalism, fault-finding, and condescension toward others. It destroys human relationships and distorts the relationship with the divine. This attitude is sternly addressed in the prophetic literature (Cf. Isaiah 5:7-25, Jeremiah 23:1, Ezekiel 13:3f., Amos 6:1) and receives much attention in the New Testament as well with regard to the religious leaders of the day (Cf. Matthew 7:1ff., 15:10ff.,

23:13ff.). Religion becomes the defense against the feeling of shame. The indictment levied against some members of the faith community is anchored in this very attitude. This defense is labeled as hypocritical because it not only masks, but falsifies, reality. Functionally, it serves to deflect one's own sense of shame and project it onto others. "I may be bad, but I'm an angel compared to . . ." is a way of articulating the phenomenon of measurement by comparison. The shame-based person finds it imperative to *always* measure over against those perceived to be inferior so as to bolster her or his own sagging or deflated self-image.

Joseph Berke has picked up on this aspect of defending against shame and writes, "The whole point is to avoid shame by becoming the shamer and making others look bad. In this way, shame and envy act in tandem. Shame rubs one's nose in the dirt, while envy rubs the dirt in one's nose."[9] Within the faith community the name of God is invoked in making these kinds of self-righteous judgments, thus increasing the impact of the shaming tactic.

Self-righteousness as a defense requires not only comparison, but demonstration. In all fairness to those who act out of this mode, more often than not they are not aware of the way in which they are perceived by others and would take great offense if they were told that they were self-righteous. The function of acting out is an attempt to have others substantiate and support the position. The intent is often blatantly obvious, as noted by Jesus in Matthew 6:1-18. The person who utilizes this religious defense for shame is also caught in a vicious circle. The shame triggers the need to feel good about the self, which is accomplished either by putting oneself forward or putting others down. Both of these tactics are considered as reprehensible by others and the individual experiences more shame. Rather than resorting to some other way of dealing with the issue, the shame-based person attempts to do more of the same and the shame cycle persists.

POWER AND CONTROL THROUGH DISGUISED MANIPULATION

Kaufman identifies striving for power and control as a major defense mechanism against shame. He says that it ". . . is a direct attempt to compensate for the sense of defectiveness which under-lies internalized shame."[10] The rationale which is employed is that one is made less vulnerable if one is in control. If I am in power or in control, it is much easier to transfer my sense of shame to another person, thus presumably eliminating any shame inducing experi-ences for myself. Hierarchical thinking and acting enters into this realm. "Wherever there are levels of power, wherever there is dis-tance in perceived power between participants in a system, there is the opportunity for shaming interaction."[11] The misuse and misap-propriation of power is experienced when such power is used as a means of shaming others in order to defend against one's own sense of shame.

Power and control may be attained in a variety of ways. For some it is striving after a social position which puts them in charge. In many instances it becomes a gender issue. In a sexist society, men believe that they have a "divine right" to wield power. There is the conviction that there is biblical evidence to support this posture of lording it over women, whether in the marriage relationship or some other setting. As a result of that belief system, exploitation can eventuate in emotional, physical, and sexual harassment, or even abuse. For others it may be subscribing to the adage which says "money talks," and therefore wealth or economics become the means whereby that person is in control. In other arenas it may be knowledge, position, skill, or some other attribute which allegedly renders that person as being in control and therefore less likely to experience the pain of shame. The biblical example which comes immediately to mind is the request of James and John in Mark 10:35-45 (For a parallel passage see Matthew 20:20-28). Desiring the positions of prestige and power is designed as much to guard against being a peasant or a peon as it is to bask in the limelight of being a celebrity.

It has been my experience within the faith community that a covert ploy to attain power is more likely to occur than an overt play for power. Members of the faith community have been schooled to be "nice" to other people, to act out the "servant" role, never to be ambitious or angry, and to shun any obvious behavior which might betray their underlying motive to exercise power and control.

In order to gain such a position of power in the community of faith, it is necessary to resort to what I would call disguised manipulation. In the parlance of psychology, it is termed passive-aggressive behavior. Since any direct seizure of power and control would be construed as unacceptable behavior to all involved, a more subtle and oftentimes more deadly approach is utilized. Even though the person's ultimate goal is to be in control, that desire must be disguised so as not to be offensive. A description of the tactics employed are what Eric Berne calls "games."[12] To play the games effectively, the person needs to know the system, the vulnerabilities of others, and devise ways to push oneself into prominence and make it appear as though no manipulation was being employed.

Typical examples of disguised manipulation include silence, withholding support, seceding from communal activities, secretiveness, and the development of covert conspiracies. These tactics are designed to instill fear, anxiety, concern, and even panic within other members of the community. An example is the person who is a major contributor to a congregation. That person likely will not demand her or his own way by overtly manipulating others through threatening to withdraw financial support. The approach will be more indirect, such as cutting back or cutting out the contributions, or absenting her or himself from worship and involvement in the community. Others will observe the behavior, interpret its import, and react accordingly by making a decision which is in conformity with what the major contributor desires. Once the community has been manipulated into doing what is desired by that person, she/he will resume and perhaps even increase contributions. No direct demands have been made, but the manipulative ploy has worked. Power and control have been maintained and the threat of shame avoided.

Divisiveness within the faith community more often than not involves what has been referred to as power struggles. The concern has to do with who is in control, who makes the decisions, who pulls the strings, who wields the power. It was not only individuals who sought such power as cited earlier in the case of James and John (Mark 10:35-45). The early church found itself in a variety of power struggles regarding the distribution of food (Acts 6), the procedure for inclusion of the Gentiles into the faith community

(Acts 15), and the advent of factionalism (I Corinthians 1:10-17). My contention is that such struggles can become vicious because control and power represent potent defense mechanisms for dealing with shame. If people are divested of power and control they are forced to face their shame and that is much too painful, so the alternative is shoring up the power position. The exercise of power may have less to do with arrogance, pride, selfishness, or haughtiness than with the fear, anxiety, and panic which comes with the threat of exposure, humiliation, and being divested of one's defense mechanism against shame. Sharing power, decision making, planning, and work may represent to the shame-based person a loss of control. Therefore tremendous amounts of time, energy, effort, and perhaps even money are expended in an attempt to remain on top.

In some faith communities the exercise of power takes the form of being "right." A person who is threatened by the prospect of shame will often go to untold lengths to prove the she/he is right, whether it has to do with policy, polity, procedures, or theology. It is fascinating to observe in the realm of theological discourse, how much of the rhetoric involved in theological disputes has to do with being right or correct or conversely proving others wrong and incorrect. The need to be right not only borders on theological idolatry, but is evidence of the sheer terror of shame should one be labeled as being wrong or incorrect. This is particularly true if a confrontation occurs in a public arena. This too may be related to a male image of domination and control. In these instances it seems imperative that one mount an argument to prove one's self right and the other person wrong. There is a smug sense of satisfaction in being able to outwit the presumed opponent and thereby feel better about one's self. The ultimate use of control in this arena is to label another person or group as being heretical and thereby, through the use of power, attempt to shame them into submission in the name of the Almighty.

Kaufman notes that power can serve two purposes. "Power becomes the means to insulate against further shame. Power can also become the means to compensate for shame internalized earlier in life."[13] As has already been demonstrated, presumed power at least gives the illusion that one is in control and therefore immune to shame. When a person experiences a power deficit she/he may attempt to compensate, as Kaufman suggests, by lusting after power so as to experience a sense of security.

As noted earlier, within the faith community, the power and control defense mechanism is often, though not always, more covert than overt. The lack of honesty and directness is often the approach. The concepts of corroboration and cooperation as evidence of colleagueship are forfeited as competitiveness and control reign supreme. Conflict and confrontation are obviously openly avoided, but the strategy of subterfuge often serves to sabotage the unity of the faith community.

THE SCAPEGOATING DEFENSE–"BLAMING"

One of the most popular ploys utilized for transferring shame is to blame others or to find a scapegoat for one's own sense of shame. Referring once again to Eric Berne, he writes that the most popular game which we as human beings play is, "If It Weren't For You."[14] Not only is guilt projected onto others, but shame is transferred as well. The inability to acknowledge and process one's own sense of shame makes it imperative to externalize it and pin it on others. Kaufman says,

> While the blaming individual escapes culpability for wrongdoing or mistakes and hence avoids shame, he reaps a harvest of discontent derived from perceived powerlessness. If the source of what goes wrong in life becomes external to the self, one has also relinquished the power to affect or alter what happens.[15]

Blaming is indicative of how powerfully shame operates in our lives. Since shame produces such pain and confrontation with one's own humanness and vulnerability, the transfer of the shame through blaming or scapegoating becomes an attractive option. If there is another person, persons, or group who will absorb the shame of others, the shame system is set in motion. Neither the blamer nor the one blamed ultimately deals with their sense of shame. Both may seemingly benefit from it in that the blamer feels that the shame has been lodged elsewhere and the one blamed may have her or his shame-based identity further substantiated. All parties are caught and entangled in a web of shame. Lansky illustrates what happens within the marital relationship when blaming is a prominent defense.

> In marriages dominated by blaming transactions, verbal conflict is characteristically at the forefront of the couple's activities. Often some transgression by a spouse serves both as a precipitant to disorganization in the blamer and a provocation to blame. Such blaming attacks may be precipitated by major transgressions or by events so small as exclusion from a conversation, or other types of seemingly mild narcissistic injury.[16]

When such blaming escalates in intensity, it can easily result in domestic violence.[17]

Within the faith community the blaming scenario takes on a variety of faces. If things are not going well and a sense of corporate shame develops, the tendency is for the community to blame the clergyperson or the congregational leadership. The clergy and/or the leaders tend to blame the laity and a vicious blaming cycle is set in motion. It is obvious that such a blaming pattern breeds an immense amount of animosity and hostility. The shame phenomenon begins to take on a life of its own within that community and continues to feed into the negative and destructive pattern. The same phenomenon can be seen at all levels of personal, corporate, and even national and international interaction.

It has been my observation that not only excessive blaming, but also excessive excusing and even excessive humor are used as defense mechanisms against shame. Those with excessive excuses betray the fact that they have the need to hide. The same can be true of the person for whom everything is a joke. As important, necessary, and salutary as humor can be, it can also become a form of distancing from others. It can create a wall of superficiality which precludes significant human relationships and interactions.

MARTYR COMPLEX

Another defense noted in the faith community is that of the martyr complex. Assuming the role of the one who is the servant of servants and slave of slaves is an attractive reinforcement for a shame-based person. One can appeal to Scriptures in order to validate the position. The servant songs of second Isaiah (42:1-4, 49:1-6, 50:4-11, 52:13, 53:12) can be cited or the oft-quoted words of Jesus with regard to servanthood, self-denial, and taking up a cross are noted (cf. Matthew 16:24 and parallels, Mark 9:33-35, 10:43-45). Does not the apostle Paul encourage such sacrifice in Romans 12:1, where he says, "I appeal to you therefore, by the mercies of God, to present your bodies as a living sacrifice, holy and acceptable to God which is your spiritual worship"? The rationale seems to be that self-effacement and self-deprecation can protect me from the shaming ploys of others. I will present myself as a one who deserves nothing in hopes that perhaps I can get something.

Contrary to the intent of these passages in Scripture which admonish servanthood for the sake of the other, the shame-based person envisions servanthood for the sake of the self. There is no real giving of the self for the sake of the neighbor; rather the motivation is to protect the self against the sting of shaming from others by "self-shaming." From that perspective, the role of servant is really self-serving! Such people are vulnerable to exploitation. Without realizing it, they send out signals to others that they are not only willing but eager to give up what they have and go the second mile whether that is appropriate or not. They will often interpret their behavior as faithfulness to the command of the Lord (Matthew 6:40-42). In essence it is not giving for the sake of giving, it is giving for the sake or protecting the self against shame.

The martyr role subtly and insidiously permeates the person's whole being and soon becomes a way of life. It is justified and validated by a misinterpretation of the religious tradition and is often rewarded by commendation.

WITHDRAWAL AND ISOLATION

"If you can't get at me, you can't shame me" is the motto of the person who uses withdrawal and isolation as a way of defending against shame. Kaufman suggests that some people have a genetic predisposition towards particular temperaments, which when nurtured by the environment become that person's defending strategy.[18] The shame may be occasioned by any one of the dynamics dealt with in the previous chapter. Withdrawal and isolation create a world of presumed safety wherein the person can hide behind seemingly impenetrable barriers erected as a fortress of defense to ward off all situations which may occasion shame. Rigidity in relationships, protectiveness of one's personal feelings, and isolation against intimacy become normative patterns of behavior. This defense represents far more than the protection against invasiveness experienced as discretionary shame or demarcation of boundaries. It is a turning in upon the self as an adaptive strategy against the pain of shame.

Avoiding vulnerability and exposure is designed to ward off any possibility of the shame experience. It obviously also precludes any joy which may ensue from a significant relationship, because such relationships require intimacy and exposure. The presumed protection of withdrawal is preferred to the possible pain of exposure. This does not mean that such a person necessarily becomes a recluse from society; rather she or he becomes an emotional recluse who carefully keeps the inner self hidden from the world.

It has been my experience in the field of chemical dependency that people within the faith community often exercise the defending strategy of withdrawal and isolation when it comes to dealing with the shame of addiction and/or abuse in the family system. Not only those afflicted with addiction and abuse, but the whole family which is affected, utilize denial, diversion, and distancing to deal with the problem. This can be observed already in children who avoid interaction with other children for fear that the family secret will somehow be disclosed. The rule is if we don't talk, don't feel, and don't act, the shame will remain hidden as a secret of the family.

Even though I have only soft data to substantiate this assertion, I believe that withdrawal and isolation can reach the point where self-abuse and self-destruction eventuate. One can feel so much shame and feel so worthless that self-abuse may be inflicted as a way of trying to exorcise the pain of shame. The ultimate action is self-destruction when the sense of disgust for the self, the sense of deficiency, being deserted, dishonored, defective, or defiled reaches monumental proportions. The person becomes overwhelmed with the sheer magnitude of the shame and death becomes the ultimate sign and form of withdrawal and isolation from the world. Leon Wurmser agrees with my thesis regarding self-destructive behavior. He says,

> A most serious problem in the treatment of these more severely shame-sick patients is the danger of suicide. The patient who is ashamed wants to disappear, never to be seen anymore. Therapy, particularly in the beginning, may mobilize so much shame that the suicidal impulses can become overwhelming. The best warning signals for the therapist are an increase of the silence, sometimes to the degree of catatonic stupor and expression of increased 'detachment.'[19]

The shame-sensitive person can lose all perspective on the world and reality and withdraw into a fantasy world ostensibly devoid of exposure and pain. Any endeavor to penetrate the walls of defense is in and of itself interpreted as an attempt to shame the person.

Kaufman summarizes his views regarding defense mechanisms by saying that the strategies develop so that the individual can avoid paralyzing shame. As the person internalizes the shame experience, it becomes evident that each succeeding experience is the occasion for either defending or transferring the shame. Exposure becomes acutely intolerable. These adaptive defenses are implemented for the sake of survival. He says that the strategies are not unitary in nature, but become ". . . expressed in most unique and varied ways, with several often learned and functioning together."[20] Defense strategies are common to all human beings who wrestle with the issue of shame. These strategies find a particularly unique and nuanced expression within the faith community. This chapter presents only a select number of defense strategies utilized to defend against shame. The reader certainly can develop her or his own list from both the personal as well as the social realm of experience.

Given the pervasiveness of the shame dynamics and the elaborate defense mechanisms employed to ward off the effects of shame, it becomes clear that for the community of faith, the issue needs to be addressed from a faith perspective. It is to this task that our attention is now drawn.

NOTES

1. Kaufman, Gershen. *Shame: The Power of Caring.* Cambridge: Schenkman Publishing Co., 1980, p. 81.
2. Kaufman, p. 82.
3. Kaufman, pp. 83-84.
4. Kaufman, p. 91.
5. Several excellent books have been written on the topic of "codependence." Only a few will be listed here.

> Beattie, Melody. *Codependent No More.* Center City, MN: Hazelden Publishing Co., 1981.
> Black, Claudia. *It Will Never Happen to Me.* Denver: M. A. C. Printing and Publications Division, 1987.
> Schaef, Anne Wilson. *Co-Dependence: Misunderstood-Mistreated.* San Francisco: Harper and Row, 1986.
> Woititz, Janet. *Adult Children of Alcoholics.* Hollywood, FL: Health Communications Inc., 1983.

6. Kaufman, p. 93.
7. Kaufman, p. 87.
8. Lewis, Helen Block. "Shame and the Narcissistic Personality." In Donald L. Nathanson (ed.), *The Many Faces of Shame.* New York: Guilford Press, 1987, p. 97.
9. Berke, Joseph H, "Shame and Envy." In Donald L. Nathanson (ed.), *The Many Faces of Shame.* New York: Guilford Press, 1987, p. 332.
10. Kaufman, p. 88.
11. Lansky, Melvin R. "Shame and Domestic Violence." In Donald L. Nathanson (ed.), *The Many Faces of Shame.* New York: Guilford Press, 1987, p. 336.
12. Berne, Eric. *The Games People Play.* New York: Grove Press, 1964.
13. Kaufman, p. 95.
14. Berne, p. 104
15. Kaufman, p. 95.
16. Lansky, p. 338.
17. Lansky, pp. 339-340.
18. Kaufman, pp. 98-99.
19. Wurmser, Leon. *The Mask of Shame.* Baltimore: Johns Hopkins University Press, 1981, p. 272.
20. Kaufman, pp. 100-101.

Chapter Five

Theological Resources from the Faith Tradition that Address the Issue of Shame

Since shame is such a powerful and pervasive force in the lives of many people, it is obviously also operative in the experience and interaction of the faith community. By its attitudes and actions, the church may exacerbate the sense of disgrace shame ensnaring its members in the web of bondage, rather than serving as a vehicle for freedom and liberation from the paralyzing and debilitating effects of shame. We utilize shame in an attempt to motivate people into action. This tactic gives rise to resentment because it is a form of manipulation. Rather than communal life being a spontaneous and celebrative response to the "good news" of liberation, the modus operandi of the faith community sometimes reveals itself as being coercive in nature. Reduced to its simplest form, the message is, "Shame on you for not doing this or not being that!" Whether it involves worship, education, stewardship, evangelism, fellowship, or any other facet of the church's corporate life, people often feel shamed into participation. Since shame is an effective coercive motivator, it is frequently employed. It is powerful enough in our daily human interactions, but when God language is introduced or invoked in conjunction with shame, most members of the faith community cave in to its incredible power. We may often experience being put on a "guilt trip," as it were, but my sense is that the "shame trip" is much more frequently used.

The faith tradition also speaks a word of liberation to those of us who suffer from the negative effects of shame. It may necessitate interpreting the tradition (in our theological reflections) from a slightly different angle or perspective, but the intent is to appropriate the message in such a way that the Word can effect freedom, not only from guilt, but also from disgrace shame. The significance of being emancipated from shame is a particularly critical concern, since guilt is rarely mentioned in the Old and New Testaments, but the Scriptures are replete with reference to shame.

CREATION-BASED THEOLOGICAL ANTHROPOLOGY

Foundational to our approach and attitude towards people is the manner in which we perceive and conceive of others. Our conceptualizations arise out of the existential concerns of any given era. Paul Tillich has suggested that the history of humankind can be roughly divided into three ages. In ancient history humans concerned themselves with the issue of fate. In the Middle Ages, the focus was on guilt. In the modern era, the issues of anxiety and meaninglessness have come to the fore.[1]

Those of us whose religious heritage stems from the Reformation of the Middle Ages have been sensitized to the reality of sin and guilt. Our theology and anthropology are reflective of that perspective in that the paradigm that we employ for dealing with the human situation is the fall-redemption model, which employs the confession, absolution, forgiveness, and restoration motif. This is a most appropriate approach for those who are burdened with the weight of guilt.

If one is dealing with a shame-based person, employing this paradigm serves only to exacerbate the sense of shame and is not effective in dealing with any guilt that may in fact underlie the sense of shame. The opening story about "Jan" is illustrative of this point. This is *not* to say that the shame-based person is no longer in need of a word of forgiving grace; rather the word of grace for the guilt which may have been incurred cannot be heard over the thunderous roar of the shame. "You do not deserve to be forgiven" is the response of the shamed voice within to a pronouncement of forgiveness. "You are a nothing," "You are not worthy of God's consideration," "You are hopeless," and "You can't even believe what you are supposed to believe" are oft-quoted phrases heard from the shame-based person. To persist with the fall-redemption paradigm dooms one to an endless cycle of futility. No amount of confession and no pronouncements of forgiveness seem to suffice or provide even a modicum of peace. The shame increases and if there is underlying guilt, it becomes even more deeply imbedded in the person's being.

For the shame-based person, beginning with an anthropology informed by creation theology, which affirms the fundamental goodness and intrinsic worth of the creature and the whole created order, is a more effective theological posture from which to operate. For those of us who work with shame-based people from the faith perspective, a whole new tone and attitude is established if the individual is viewed and begins to view her or himself as a priceless person in the eyes of God and others who is endowed with unique and special gifts and talents. This is not to soft-pedal, ignore, or obviate the reality of sin with its various expressions of pride, rebellion, thwarting the will of God, and all of the other acts which contribute to the brokenness of the human situation. Rather it is to suggest that when dealing with the phenomenon of shame, it is helpful to reframe one's anthropology in the light of creation theology. The priestly account of creation in Genesis does state unequivocally that God looked at what had been created and said, "Behold, it is very good" (Genesis 1:31). In other words, there is intrinsic value in creation and its materiality precisely because it is a creation of God. Yet many of the issues involving shame have to do with that which is material or embodied.

Unfortunately, many within the faith community have succumbed to the gnostic heresy that elevates the importance of the nonmaterial and relegates that which is material to the realm of evil. Yet it is clear that God is very much involved with the created order as evidenced by the metaphors from nature used to speak about the close relationship between God and the created world. For example, the righteous person is compared to a tree in Psalm 1:3, the disciples of Jesus are referred to as branches on a vine in John 15, and repeatedly God's people are referred to as sheep with the Lord as their shepherd (Psalm 23, 100, John 10, etc.). There is a metaphorical as well as an incarnational linkage with creation which, as the Apostle Paul states in Romans 1:20, reveals the very nature of God. The heart and center of Christian theology affirms the incarnation as pivotal (John 1:1-18, Philippians 2:5-11). The church catholic, in its ancient creeds, speaks of the "resurrection of the body" rather

than the immortality of the soul. God is not only linked with materiality and corporeality, but is also incarnated in human flesh. This
reality has important consequences for the people of God as they
deal with shame issues.

As Martin Klopfenstein has pointed out, shame is often linked
with sexuality.[2] Because of the devaluation of that which is material, embodiment has historically created problems for members of
the faith community. Much shaming is fixated on that which is
associated with the body and sexuality. The word "flesh" (*sarx* in
Greek) has become almost exclusively associated with sexuality in
the duality of spirit and body, rather than representing that which is
antithetical to the will of God. As a result, celibacy and virginity
have historically been lifted up as preferred states of religious existence. In his research on sexuality and shame, Silvan Tomkins has
come to this conclusion with regard to the ethos which Christianity
has created in relationship to sexuality:

> When we move to the Christian conception of sexuality and
> shame we move to a pluralism of ideologies and sectarian
> controversies, as in most religions. It is, however, clear that
> sexuality and shame become primarily moral and religious
> matters. Sexuality became one among many marks of the hu-
> man being's fall from innocence and from love of and by God,
> for which s/he lived in the shadow of eternal damnation. Not
> only has sexuality turned from shame to guilt, but a massive
> burden of terror has been added to the sexual act. Sexuality is
> no longer aesthetic or unaesthetic, platonic or illusory, a threat
> to the active, honorable political life, a threat to the reproduc-
> tion of the species and to the monogamous family, nor a threat
> to the will of the individual; it is now above all else a sign of
> disobedience to the will of God, demanding that the individual
> risk a variety of punishments, including an eternity in Hell.
> Shame and terror are now tightly fused.[3]

From infancy, strong messages are overtly and covertly given
regarding the body. The genitals are associated with that which is
"dirty" or "unclean." Some researches believe that " . . . a major
source of shame during the toddler period is the 'negative reaction

of a parent who looks on the infant anxiously when the child is engaged in genital exploration or play.' "[4]

The hygienic concerns of the Old Testament that refer to female menstruation as the time of "uncleanness" and "impurity" contribute to the negative attitudes associated with sexuality and sexual functioning. While that may not have been the original intent, nonetheless, the language in and of itself connotes shame. Likewise, the rather peculiar pericope in Mark 5:27-34 which recounts the narrative of the woman with the flow of blood may be instructive at this point. She certainly was aware of all the hygienic laws regarding her situation. It was likely the shame of her impurity which prevented her from addressing Jesus directly with regard to her plight. So she sneaks up on him, in order that she might be healed and free from this curse of shame which had plagued her for so long. She could not approach him face to face, for that would accentuate her sense of shame regarding her situation and condition.

It is also evident that in the hierarchy of sins that has been constructed by the church that the sins associated with the body seem to receive the most attention, whether it be lust, fornication, or adultery. The persistent sins of the spirit such as envy, jealousy, slander, hatred, and judgmentalism, which slay the spirit within others, are often ignored. This negative emphasis is the genesis for much shame associated with the body and its functions.

A positive and healthy emphasis upon a doctrine of the goodness of creation creates a more suitable context and environment for relating to the shame-based person. The cognitive acknowledgement of this truth is not sufficient to persuade the shame-based person to change her or his attitude. It is an attitude which is caught rather than taught as the shame-based person slowly begins to alter her or his self-perception. As will be noted later, this occurs through association with others who have a healthy self-image and through intentional efforts that serve to substantiate this reality.

The Pauline metaphor of the body as the "temple of the Holy Spirit" (I Corinthians 3:16-17) is a helpful image for the shame-based person. It emphasizes not only the sacredness of embodied life, but also the value that God places upon the creatures whom God has created. There is intrinsic value in "being" because each person has been created in love. To quote an old adage, "God does not make junk!" A unilateral anthropology which focuses exclusively upon sin, evil, and fallenness drives the shame-based person into deeper despair. Unfortunately, despair does not in desperation give way to grace and mercy, but fosters only greater hopelessness and shame. The shame which creates the sense of worthlessness, self-deprecation, and meaninglessness must first be dealt with before the merciful word of forgiving grace for one's sin and guilt can be heard and appropriated.

Creation theology enjoins the members of the faith community to adhere to the two great commandments of love quoted by Jesus (Matthew 22:37 par.). Love for God results in love of neighbor, self, and the rest of the created order. In my judgment, hate of self results also in hating God, others, and the rest of the created order. Self-hate which arises out of a pronounced sense of shame is not conducive to establishing healthy relationships with God, others, or nature. In other words, the equation works in both directions. Love begets more love, hate begets more hate, and shame begets more shame. The shame issue is not only a personal and private matter. It has far-reaching implications for our relationship with God, others, and nature. It has often been said that it is a shame the way we treat other people and our environment or the world of nature. Perhaps those shameful relationships are engendered in large part by our own shame-based identities. If one sees little or no value or worth in oneself, that attitude will inevitably be reflected in our relationships to the rest of reality.

Many people in the faith community still view themselves as being "totally depraved." While the theological intent of this idea was to acknowledge the distinction between the Creator and the creature, it has been construed by many in the faith community as meaning that the image of God has been totally effaced in humankind, or that there is absolutely no worth or value associated with that which is human. This perception on the part of people serves to accentuate the impact of disgrace shame. Even as claiming equality with God is a distorted understanding of what it means to be human, so also is total disconnectedness with God as Creator also a distortion of what it means to be human. A more balanced anthropology which appeals to the fundamental worth and value of creation and its eternal connection with God is a necessary antidote for the poison of disgrace shame which plagues many people.

AN ACKNOWLEDGEMENT
AND ACCEPTANCE OF FINITUDE

Closely connected with an anthropology which acknowledges the goodness of the created order and, more specifically, existence in the flesh, is a parallel acceptance of finitude as the nature of human existence. Simply and plainly stated, creatureliness, with all of its limitations, is a given for all human beings. The shame-based person has been led to believe and has emotionally internalized quite a different message. The deeply imbedded assumption and presupposition is that one is intrinsically worthless if saddled with natural human limitations. There is an obvious paradox and dilemma which faces the shame-based-person. The rationale may be irrational, nonetheless, the process follows a particular pattern. Acceptability as a person to others and oneself is predicated on achievement by doing things perfectly. Perfection implies operating without limitation. Even though the shame-based person may cognitively acknowledge the reality of limitation and finitude, she or he cannot appropriate that emotionally and spiritually. Exposure of one's limitations is interpreted by the shame-based person as probable cause for rejection, which spells unacceptability. Therefore, incredible time and energy is consumed in covering up, hiding, or masking one's limitations as a human being.

The impossibility of the situation does not preclude repeated attempts and demands to live as though there were no limitations. The shame-based person is like an individual attempting to walk on water. The assumption is that it should be possible and therefore failure to do so results in anxiety about being rejected by others and being found unacceptable. The illogical and irrational nature of the situation does not prevent the person from attempting and expecting to do the impossible.

If one is to speak about the nature of sin to the shame-based person, it is within this context. The shame-based person feels compelled to exceed the limits of finitude and in so doing confuses the creature with the Creator. In our essence as human beings we are limited and we cannot transcend the bounds of space, time, or human capability. Even if the faulty assumption system is pointed out, this in and of itself does not release the shame-based person from the dilemma. It must be remembered that for most shame-based adults, the assumption system is deeply imbedded in the person's being. Reprimand for assuming the place of God is not a helpful strategy; that only exacerbates the sense of shame.

As a pastor I can recall my frustration in attempting to convince a counselee that the assumptions and self-expectations were unrealistic. My point was that we are not God and we ought not conduct ourselves as though we were and judge ourselves accordingly. The more I tried to persuade the individual, the more resolute became the defenses against my rational pleas. It requires more than logic or argumentation to shift the assumption system so that it embraces reality. Further discussion of this most difficult situation will be addressed in the final chapter.

The community of faith individually and corporately needs to speak truthfully and candidly about finitude and its implied limitations. The sense of shame as deficiency is often the result of pious expectations and messages which predicate acceptability on the basis of perfect adherence to prescribed codes of conduct. The individual's energy becomes totally consumed by this fastidious attention to personal conduct. The end result is egocentrism as the person becomes curved in upon the self (*In curvatus se*). It is critical to recognize that this is *not* a life-style which is intentionally chosen, rather it is an adaptive life-style which is utilized in an attempt to deal with the power of shame in that person's life. To denounce and condemn this kind of narcissistic disposition only increases the shame.

The task is to learn to celebrate the limitations of human existence. Human finitude is not a curse. It is a gift which frees us from the anxiety of having to be like God! Yet as a faith community in our proclamation and expectations of ourselves and one another, we often undergird the assumption system of many shame-based people by giving the impression that perfection is a possibility.

In recent years the so-called human potentials movement has in its own way attempted to lift up the positive aspects of human possibility and potential. This was a laudable shift from the pathological focus that predominated for so long. It is not, however, without its own pitfalls. The shame-based person interprets this approach not as a challenge to move from mediocrity to maximizing her or his potential; rather the situation is construed as another "should" which has been mandated. In addition to that, there are no boundaries or limits established with regard to potentiality. Establishing impossible goals only feeds the shame cycle of frustration and failure. What is intended as a positive focus in the human potentials movement ends up as a negative and a curse for the shame-based person. It is difficult if not impossible for the shamed person to utter the Pauline statement about being content in whatever state or situation one might be (Philippians 4:11). Even the best is not good enough.

It seems imperative in our preaching and teaching that the issue of finitude and its implied limitations also be addressed, as a way of alerting the shame-based people in the community of faith that there is a more salutary way of dealing with shame other than striving for perfection. This attitude detracts from community because the preoccupation is with the self. It also precludes the gifts of spontaneity, joy, and peace which are promised to those who are claimed by God. Perhaps the simplest guide I have found to deal with the issue of finitude is found in the words of the Serenity Prayer.

God, grant me the serenity to accept the things I cannot change, courage to change the things I can, and the wisdom to know the difference. Amen

BAPTISM AS THE SOURCE OF IDENTITY

Kaufman,[5] Lynd,[6] and others have stressed the significance of people developing a shame identity from infancy throughout their development. Erik Erikson addresses the issue of shame in his epigenetic schema of human development as one of the early crises to be resolved.[7] He sees the development of an identity as primarily an adolescent task.[8] If the second epigenetic stage of autonomy versus shame and doubt is not resolved, chances are that the task of establishing an identity later in life will be shame-based. A lack of clear identity coupled with the perception of the shame-based person that she/he is without worth, value, and significance establishes the foundation for a lifelong shame-based identity. This disposition affects not only the conceptualization of the self, but also has an impact on relationships with others.

The community of faith confesses that one's identity is something which is covenantally established from without by God. The concept of covenant is a central unifying theme that runs throughout the Old and New Testaments. The Old Testament rite of circumcision was a visible sign of the covenant relationship between God and the people of Israel. In the New Testament, the initiation into the community is accomplished through baptism. In each of these instances the covenant is a unilateral action of God's unqualified grace freely given to the community. In and through the covenant relationship the individual and/or group is provided with an identity. The issue of establishing an identity is accomplished in a number of ways.

The baptismal covenant is often associated with the giving of a name which becomes that person's identity. Second Isaiah says, "I have called you by name, you are mine" (Isaiah 43:1). The Old Testament is replete with instances where naming is critically important as noted by Pedersen.[9] According to Pedersen, the name was more than a means of identification for an individual, as it was believed that the name actually carried with it the essence of that person's being. Therefore one's "name" was not to be taken lightly. It was sacred and carried powers all its own. The name was so significant that momentous occasions are often marked by the changing of the name to memorialize the occasion. For example, in Genesis 17:5, the name Abram which means "exalted father," is changed to Abraham, which means "father of a multitude." The name becomes descriptive of the purpose that Abraham has in the divine plan, namely that he and his wife Sarah (whose name was also changed in Genesis 17:15) shall be the forebears of the chosen people who will inhabit the promised land. (Note the significance of the name change in Genesis 32:28-30, Matthew 16:17-18, and Acts 13:9.)

More recent scholarship in the area of dealing with the use of name in the Old Testament has been provided by George W. Ramsey, who associates the utilization of "name" with the issue of discernment as opposed to earlier interpretations dealing with dominance.[10]

The naming ceremony in conjunction with the sign of the covenant continues in the Jesus story of the New Testament (Luke 2:21). It is ultimately the name of Jesus which the Christian community holds up as central for its salvific proclamation (Acts 4:12). In its eschatological hope, the faith community images its reality in terms of the names of the saints having been written in the book of life (Philippians 4:3, Revelation 17:8, 20:12, 21:27). With the name given in the covenantal act of baptism, an identity is also imparted which is not a shame-based identity, but one which is sanctified by the God whose will it is to be in covenant relationship with all people.

One's identity is further noted within the faith community as baptism "sealing" that person into a specific caring community. The writer of Ephesians picks up on this particular motif in Ephesians 1:13 and 4:30 when he speaks about being sealed with the Holy Spirit, a gift which is given through baptism. The reality of being claimed, sealed, and kept through the covenantal relationship with God provides the certainty of inclusion and acceptance which is so desperately needed by the shame-based person. The shamed person fears rejection and exclusion leaving her or him deserted and abandoned. The faith tradition offers an unconditional acceptance and inclusion accomplished by the covenantal relationship established by God with that person, rather than the person feeling that this responsibility for acceptance resides exclusively with her or him.

Finally in the Christian tradition, the identity issue is related to oneness with the crucified and risen Christ. The Apostle Paul says,

Do you not know that all of us who have been baptized into Christ Jesus were baptized into his death? We were buried therefore with him by baptism into death, so that as Christ was raised from the dead by the glory of the Father, we too might walk in newness of life. (Romans 6:3–4).

Furthermore, "For as many of you as were baptized into Christ have put on Christ" (Galatians 3:27). The import of these texts suggests that the baptized member of the faith community has her or his whole past, present, and future inextricably bound up with Christ Jesus. This would suggest that we do not find our identity, but rather our identity has been given to us and is found in the gracious work of God.

This truth lifts the burden of searching for an identity on our own. More often than not, the identity which we find on our own is shame-based. The responsibility on the part of parents and the community of faith is to impart and instill this reality in the minds and hearts of children. The child's identity has been already determined by a covenantal act of God, whether that be circumcision, baptism, or some other ceremony whereby the religious community incorporates others into its fellowship. The person is given an identity and is accepted as one who belongs in this community. Identity involves belonging to a given group. In tandem, identity and belonging spell acceptance, which is a key ingredient in dealing with shame.

The sign of the covenant is a daily reminder to the community of faith not only who we are, but whose we are, for we have been named and claimed through the gracious promise of God and held safely and securely. The biblical image of the Shepherd and the sheep serves well to illustrate this reality (John 10; note specifically verses 28 and 29). The deep human need for acceptance, belonging, identity, and incorporation is provided for in the community's covenantal relationship with God.

One other aspect of baptism is also important for the shame-based person who suffers from the sense of being dirty or defiled. Several biblical texts refer to baptism as the cleansing or washing ritual which removes any sense of stain or impurity. The concern for cleansing and purity is a well-documented concept in the Old Testament, with ritual prescriptions provided to accomplish this fact. The New Testament is likewise replete with references to the need for cleansing, whether it be from leprosy or some other form of impurity (e.g., Matthew 8:2, 10:8, 11:5, and parallels). The whole scenario in Acts 10 is an effort to obliterate the practice of exclusivity based on ritual law. What God has declared as clean is not to be considered as unclean (Acts 10:15-16; note its implications in Acts 10:34ff and 11:1-18). The cleansing power provided in the waters of baptism is noted in Ephesians 5:26 and also in Titus 3:5. Any real or perceived stain, impurity, or uncleanness is unilaterally removed by the gracious action of God. The baptismal message is that you are cleansed.

The relevance of this reality for the shame-based person is immediately apparent, whether the shame has to do with identity, inclusion, acceptance, or cleansing. The theology of the covenant as established in baptism provides a rich resource from the faith tradition for addressing the issues of shame.

GRACE AS ACCEPTANCE

While the guilt-laden person needs to interpret and experience grace as a word of forgiveness and pardon for culpability, the shame-based person requires an experiential encounter with grace as unconditional acceptance. Accept that you are accepted is Paul Tillich's succinct summary of the Gospel message of God's grace, and this epitomizes the need of the shame-based person.[11] Grace is the antidote for the venom of disgrace shame. It is the sole cure for the metastasizing malignancy within individuals and groups who are plagued with shame. Unacceptability and being labeled as unlovable govern the shame-based person's self-image, actions, and determine her or his attitudes toward the self, others, and the world. Emancipation from the bondage of shame through the grace of acceptance may be the initial course of action and concern before grace as a word of forgiveness can be heard and appropriated.

The faith tradition has affirmed from time immemorial that God in grace continues in steadfast love (hesed in Hebrew) to embrace the community of faith even when the community has been unfaithful to the covenant relationship. Whereas the community and individuals within the community engage in behavior which is unacceptable and incur guilt which needs to be confessed, the community is not shamefully deserted and abandoned by God. Despite its blatant rebellion and rejection of God, God is determined not to be frustrated and will preserve, if nothing more, at least a remnant as a sign that the promise of faithfulness will never be broken (Isaiah 10:20-22, 11:10-16, Jeremiah 23:3, 31:7, Romans 11:5). The persistence of God in relationship to the covenant community and its individual members is an eternal sign of grace which is freely granted. The ultimate experience of shame would be to be deserted and abandoned by God, a divine sign of unacceptability.

It is this word of acceptability and the promise that the person will not be abandoned which constitutes the critical importance of grace for the shame-based person. Intellectual acceptance and verbal affirmation normally do not carry sufficient power or weight for the shame-based person to shift her or his personal attitude. Grace must be incarnationally experienced. A case scenario may be most illustrative.

"Jenny" seemed to be suffering from a variety of physical, emotional, and spiritual maladies when she came for a consultation about her situation. After several sessions it seemed that there was little or no progress in overcoming her feelings. She seemed resolutely tied to her own low self-image, refused to try anything new, and was resistive to my efforts to make a connection with her. She continued to return for sessions repeatedly, but the relationship seemed to be an exercise in frustration and futility. I realized that she was a deeply shamed person and had developed elaborate defenses to guard against any further pain. On several occasions she suggested that she just "give up" because nothing was going to do any good or help anyway.

We began to address her attitude of giving up and discovered that such a tactic indicated two things. First of all, it confirmed her own self-image and understanding that she was unacceptable and giving up was a symbol of desertion and abandonment which further substantiated her own shame. Second, she finally admitted that if she became truly honest and shared of herself that I would reject her because she felt that she was in essence a worthless person who did not deserve to be accepted, helped, or loved. She actually believed she was so worthless that contact with other human beings would infect or contaminate them with her shame, so withdrawal and isolation became additional defenses to break through. She desperately wanted and needed to be significantly related to another person, but her shame sabotaged all efforts in that direction. It took several months of persistent patience before a breakthrough occurred and she began to believe that she was accepted by at least one person in the world for who she was and not for what she might or should be.

Grace for the shame-based person requires an incarnational experience of unconditional acceptance. Gershen Kaufman refers to this in psychological and relational terms as establishing the "interpersonal bridge."[12] Connectedness with another person provides the path leading to self-acceptance and the awareness that by grace one is also acceptable to God.

It was this kind of self-acceptance through grace which is evident in the statement of St. Paul, "But by the grace of God I am what I am, and his grace toward me was not in vain" (I Corinthians 15:10). Paul was able to accept his sense of unacceptability and thereby experience the grace of unconditional acceptance and love. This was not only a cognitive fact, but an experiential encounter which was not only eschatologically salvific, but also provided purpose and meaning for his temporal existence. The centrality of grace in the life of Paul enabled him to embrace his humanity with all of its limitations including the sense of weakness or impotency in the face of overwhelming odds. His statement in II Corinthians 12:9 about God's grace in the face of his own pain and limitations is eloquently stated as the Lord says to him, "My grace is sufficient for you, for my power is made perfect in weakness." The natural tendency for the shame-based person is to deny the pain, hide the reality and feelings of weakness, and erect strong defenses as a way of remaining safe, secure, and secretly harboring the shame. The message of grace serves to turn this disposition on its head. Paul is so bold as to say that living by the grace of God "I will all the more gladly boast of my weaknesses, that the power of Christ may rest upon me. For the sake of Christ, then, I am content with weaknesses, insults, hardships, persecutions, and calamities; for when I am weak, then I am strong" (II Corinthians 12:9-10). Note that in the catalogue of circumstances cited by Paul, all are shame-inducing situations. Exposure of weakness, being insulted, experiencing disadvantage through hardship, being subject to persecution, and all other experiences of human calamity evoke powerful feelings of shame. The good news of grace is that this is all overcome. The humiliation of disgrace shame is transformed into a victorious revelation of God's grace that enables the person not only to accept her or his unacceptability as disgustingly human and weak, but even to boast and revel in this weakness as a further witness to the power of God's grace. The centrality of grace in Pauline theology is applicable not only in terms of release from guilt, but also release from the shame of self-disgust, deficiency, dishonor, defectiveness, desertion, and defilement. God's unilateral declaration of grace is one of acceptability and love. If this message can be translated experientially in the lives of shame-based people, release and newness of life can result.

JUSTIFICATION

The heart of Reformation theology has been lodged in the Pauline declaration of justification by grace through faith. Traditionally forensic categories have been employed to interpret the doctrine of justification. Whether it be the imagery of the law court, the idea of ransom or rescue, or the concept of expiation, the interpretation in large part has been focused on dealing with the matter of guilt. In his classical work on atonement, Gustaf Aulen has delineated for us the various theories designed to explicate the matter of how one becomes reconciled to God or moves to atonement with God. This interpretation is a logical extension of the Old Testament concept of sacrifice for sin. As Aulen points out, its Christological appropriation has taken on a variety of theological theories to indicate how sin as the barrier between God and humankind is overcome.[13]

This is indeed a freeing message for the guilt-ridden person. As has already been stated, the confession, absolution, forgiveness, and reconciliation paradigm is appropriate, but for the person who is dealing with shame, the doctrine of justification necessitates a different perspective. More often than not, the shame-based person is not dealing with unethical or immoral behavior. Rather, this person is struggling with the issue of "saving face," "projecting an ideal image," and "protecting the self" from the pain of shame. The method for doing so as pointed out in the last chapter is to develop strong defense mechanisms or, to put it in a theological category, it is a matter of "self-justification." The guilt-ridden person attempts to "pay" for the guilty behavior by engaging in "make-up" activity, which is designed to overcome the relational breach with God, others, the self, and nature through work, hence, the concern for "works righteousness" as a self-styled path to salvation. The shame-based person, on the other hand, engages in developing strategies which either defend or transfer the pain of shame. The issue and intent of self-justification for the shamed person is not works righteousness to "make up" for sin, but falsification and misrepresentation to "make over" or to mask the self.

As has been noted previously, the person may or may not have underlying guilt issues to address. Oftentimes guilt and shame are so inextricably bound together that they are difficult to separate, but it is my sense that this ontological sense of shame having to do with one's person takes precedence over the phenomenological sense of guilt occasioned by transgression of the person's moral or ethical code. One can sense the difference in the emphasis which the person may make when speaking about her or himself. The guilty person will say, "I did *that*" with a focus on the behavior. The shame-based person will say "*I* did that" with an emphasis upon the "I." The differentiation may be subtle, but significant.

The shame-based person engages in developing, refining, and employing strategies to deny, distance, deflect, or defer the shame. The focal point of concern is not defending behavior, but rather defending the self! Some of these self-justifying strategies were considered in the last chapter.

The word of liberation for the shame-based person coming from the doctrine of justification is that God has declared to you that you are a person of value and worth. Expending energy and effort in creatively attempting to justify one's existence is not only futile, but unnecessary. The very fact that you are created as a child of God in and of itself is sufficient justification for your existence. As noted earlier, if justifying one's existence becomes the singular focus of life, the person inevitably becomes turned in on the self. There remains no time or energy to invest on behalf of the neighbor. Shame creates lack of love and acceptance of the self. The wisdom of the dominical injunction to love one's neighbor *as oneself* (Mark 12:31, 33 par.) can be seen in its fullness when considering the saying from the negative perspective; namely, that you cannot love your neighbor if you do not love yourself! The shame-based person feels not only unloved, but loveless. When there is no sense of love, there can be no sense of value or worth. Shame, therefore, makes it imperative for the person to attempt to justify her or himself by employing defending and deflecting strategies in order to justify her or his existence.

Liberation from the stranglehold of shame which virtually compels people to engage in self-justifying tactics, and experience of the freedom of being who one is created to be, loved for what one is, and valued because one has been given the gift of life by God, is critical for the shame-based person. Self-fixing and self-fixation must be transformed into an awareness and appropriation of the divine decree that one's existence is justified by virtue of one's being created, redeemed, and sustained by God.

That reality can be appropriated only in faith. Faith is not defined here as an intellectual assent to a given set of dogmatic propositions, but rather as an unqualified trust in a gracious, merciful, and loving God who suffers with people in the midst of their pain. Theologically for the shame-based person, the gift of faith must be physically, intellectually, emotionally, and spiritually appropriated in such a way that there is a radical reversal in self-perception based on the justifying Word of God. The person not only believes (cognitively) but experiences (affectively) that engaging in self-justifying behavior through the development of elaborate self-defense strategies is no longer necessary. The message is that you have become through God's grace a "new being" whose existence, identity, worth, and value are already guaranteed and determined.

Obviously the aforementioned process is easier said than done! Oftentimes an idea or process looks good on paper, but its implementation is quite another matter. Faith in this context in essence means a trust that enables the person to make an unconditional surrender. It is not easy to surrender the elaborate defense mechanisms so carefully constructed over the years. It is not easy to surrender absolute control of one's life and entrust God with the past, present, and future. The concluding chapter will deal more specifically with the process whereby one can begin to be emancipated from the debilitating and paralyzing effects of disgrace shame.

THE CROSS AS GOD'S SHAME-BEARING SYMBOL

The Christian faith has traditionally considered the cross as the central symbol for its understanding of God's love for the world.

Using the language of justification, the cross symbolizes God's identification and participation in the human arena and represents the divine action whereby the world is redeemed from sin and death. This is certainly the most prominent interpretation in New Testament theology. The cross of Christ is the instrument of his death, but it is instrumental in effecting the salvation of humankind.

There is another perspective, less emphasized and known, wherein the tradition also speaks of the cross as God's shame-bearing symbol in behalf of the world. Particularly instructive is the conviction of the writer of Hebrews, who speaks not only of God bearing the sin of the world upon the cross, but also of the shame of the world being borne in cruciform. Hebrews 12:2 admonishes the faithful to look to Jesus, ". . . the pioneer and perfecter of our faith who for the joy that was set before him endured the cross, despising the shame." The shame incurred through death by crucifixion has many implications. Paul in Galatians 3:13 connects it with the "curse" of God as noted in the deuteronomic tradition (Deuteronomy 21:22-23). Earlier, in Galatians 3:1, Paul characterizes Christ as being "publicly portrayed" as crucified. In keeping with Roman custom, many who were crucified were nakedly exposed before the whole world as dying an ignominious death. They experienced not only the excruciating physical pain which accompanied crucifixion, but also the pain of public exposure, derision, ridicule, contempt, and mockery (Luke 23:35-39 and par.). These are all adjectives which are descriptive of the shame experience. Thus an important point of divine identification regarding the shame of humiliation, despair, failure, and defeat is experienced.

In tracing the ministry of Jesus through the Gospel narratives, I am struck by the plethora of encounters which involve shame situations. The circumstances surrounding his birth, according to the account in Matthew's gospel, involves the issue of shame. When it is discovered that Mary is pregnant, ". . . her husband Joseph, being a just man and unwilling to put her to shame, resolved to divorce her quietly" (Matthew 1:19). The shame of the situation prompted Joseph to consider quietly divorcing Mary rather than subject her to suffering exposure. An act of divine intervention precludes his need for face-saving action. Jesus' frequent confrontation, with his adversaries during the course of his public ministry often involve shame tactics. Attempts are made to cast aspersions on his author-ity, authenticity, and activities. The epitome of shame is the accusa-tion levied against him that he is in fact in league with the demonic powers of darkness (Matthew 12:24). The implication for his fol-lowers is that they can expect similar shameful treatment (Matthew 5:11, 10:25, etc.).

The passion account presents a collage of shaming experiences for Jesus. Despite the alleged triumphal entry into Jerusalem, the scenario in fact presents a caricature of what constitutes a conquer-ing monarch. The betrayal by Judas and later abandonment by his disciples are deeply shame-inducing experiences. His appearances before Herod and Pilate are filled with shame. The false accusations and indictment, the scourging, the derision and mockery of the robe and crown of thorns, as well as the clamoring demands and jeers of the mob, are all indicators of shame. Carrying his own cross and being crucified "outside the city walls" (Hebrews 13:13), coupled with the public exposure of his pain, which is heightened by deri-sion, mockery, and total humiliation, are all designed to intensify the sense of shame. Leon Wurmser makes this observation concern-ing the experience of shame.

> The punishing actions of shaming usually consist in exposing the person even more, holding him up in the pillory to the mockery of the public. Every bit of his shamefulness and ignominy is dragged into the light of day and exposed to public derision, because "laughter kills."[14]

Even though Wurmser certainly did not have the crucifixion in mind when he penned those words, they nonetheless describe in part what the experience of the cross must have been. The cross represents to the world the epitome of failure, defeat, and desertion. The sense of desertion is so great that the despairing cry from the cross is, "My God, my God, why have you forsaken me?" (Matthew 27:46).

Christological formulations which assert the sinlessness of Christ may call into question from a human perspective his ability to truly understand the pangs of guilt which plague humankind, but the pain of shame was a constant companion throughout his life, ministry, and death. The incarnation provides the intersection of identifica-tion of the divine with the human situation and condition.

The expectation of being externally subjected to shaming situations is a given in the life of faith. It is part of the "cross-bearing" life-style. However, the external shame is not to be internalized so that one becomes ashamed of the Christ or of the Gospel. "For whoever is ashamed of me and my words in this adulterous and sinful generation, of him will the Son of man also be ashamed, when he comes in the glory of his Father with the holy angels" (Mark 8:38 and par.). The Apostle Paul emphatically states, "For I am not ashamed of the gospel. . ." (Romans 1:16). External shaming is to be expected, but personalized internal shame or embarrassment which might be experienced as a result of claiming or proclaiming the Christ and his message has serious consequences.

The cross as God's shame-bearing symbol is a word of good news for the shame-based person. It celebrates the incarnational identification which God in Christ has with the shame-based person. A word of liberation from the debilitating effects of disgrace shame is announced through the message of the cross. Once again, a cognitive affirmation of this truth is not in and of itself sufficient to break the chains of shame. The power of the message must be experientially and emotionally appropriated so that the person is emancipated from the paralyzing effects of shame.

THE COMMUNITY OF FAITH

The very nature and constitution of the faith community itself can be a vital resource for dealing with shame. The shame-based person is confronted with a perplexing paradox. There is a deep inner need for relatedness, connectedness, and acceptance which comes about only by communal contact and participation. For shame-based persons, other people often represent a threat and stimulate their anxiety and fear of further exposure and shaming. This prompts the person to protectively withdraw once again into the safe confines of her or his fortress of defenses. Mobilizing the resources of the faith community in such a way that the shame-based person will utilize the benefits they provide is the key to healthy communal existence.

The Pauline injunction to "bear one another's burdens and so fulfill the law of Christ" (Galatians 6:2) is an important maxim for the faith community which desires to minister effectively to shame-based people. The burdens that believers bear are multiple in shape and form, but the burden of shame shouldered by countless people begs for mutual bearing and sharing.

The key ingredient necessary for the shame-based person in the community of faith is genuine fellowship. Gershen Kaufman believes that there is an ongoing quest for belonging, for being a part of a community, and that various pursuits are undertaken in order to fulfill that basic human need. He says,

> The need to belong to something larger than ourselves underlies many of these pursuits. We long to feel a vital part of some community of others, to have the security that comes through belonging to something larger than ourselves. It is through identification that ultimately we know rootedness.[15]

The tendency of deeply shamed people, as has already been noted, is to seek isolation. The debilitating effects of shame are overcome only through relationships, which implies community. In order for the shame-based person to enter into the corporate life of the community, it is imperative that the community posture itself in such a way that it is open and inviting. A healthy communal life is one in which grace as acceptance is practiced and mutual disclosure is made possible by faith as trust in the group itself. Judgmentalism, elitism, exclusivity, and pretentious piety are attitudes that preclude participation by the shame-based person. An environment of trust and mutuality must be established which invites and serves as a model of what it means to embrace the totality of one's humanity. The grace of acceptance and the love demonstrated by the group creates a safe place in which to share one's shame as well as guilt and find hope, healing, and health in the process.

The community of faith is a community of prayer. The salutary benefits of corporate prayer for the people of God have been well documented in the Scriptures as well as in the history of the church. The tabernacle in the Old Testament became the focal point of nomadic Israel where the worship of sacrifice and prayer could be made. King Solomon, in his dedicatory prayer, indicates that the temple is to be a place of prayer where the concerns and crises of the people can be articulated before Yahweh (I Kings 8:22-53). The establishment of the community of faith in the New Testament is centered around four basic activities: devotion to the apostle's teaching, fellowship, the breaking of bread, and prayers (Acts 2:42). This description of the early community suggests that study (the devotion to the apostles' teaching) was a key ingredient in the establishment of community. In this setting, study involves dialogue. Attention is given to the substantive issues in the life of the community and the discourse within the community becomes an important factor in the establishment of corporate and personal identity.

Fellowship implies interaction. It has been established that isolation and withdrawal are primary defenses utilized in defending against shame. *Koinoia,* which is the Greek word used in this text from Acts 2:42, implies the establishment of close relationships or intimate relationships. Fellowship is a sign of solidarity, a participation and sharing with others. The faith community can therefore be a primary resource for contact within the context of concern and care.

The breaking of bread likely refers to the sacramental fellowship which the community shared in the eucharist. It has been determined that before the eucharist was celebrated that the community shared in the *agape* or love feast, wherein the sharing, eating, and drinking of food and beverage served to encourage and foster relationships.

Prayer was a vital force in bonding the community together. Its power as a healing agent from shame will be dealt with in more detail in the next chapter.

The faith community also offers the corporate experience of worship in which the shame-based person is invited to participate. One of the unique things about worship is that it is "other-directed," rather than being primarily inner-directed. That is to say, the focus of attention is shifted from the self to God. The hymns of praise and prayer are offered by the community to the God who has created, redeemed, and sustained them. This upward and outward movement of expression has a concomitant uplifting effect for the participants as well. I found it important for shame-based people to have this kind of corporate experience which is other-directed as a way of shifting the focus of attention from the self.

The faith community likewise relies upon its rites and rituals as a way of establishing and maintaining solidarity. Most significant in many communions is the celebration of the Eucharist. The theological interpretation of the nature and purpose of this ritual varies from communion to communion, but functionally it serves to connect the individual as well as the group with God and with one another. The value of this kind of connectedness for those who feel disconnected is inestimable. For the shame-based person it can concretize an action of acceptance with one's shame, as well as being the medium of forgiveness for one's guilt. In the acts of eating and drinking, the participants are engaged in a communal experience of mercy and grace. An assurance of acceptability coupled with the promise of new life presents the shame-based person with a most precious gift.

In a society which stresses individualism and places extreme pressure upon persons to prove their worth and value, the faith community can serve as a haven from such daily demands. The community confesses that its source of life, worth, value, and importance comes from its Creator, that is One who is outside of the self. The community symbolizes human solidarity, gracious acceptance, mutual celebration of rites and rituals, as well as the matrix in which healing, health, and hope can be realized.

Each person or faith community can likely identify other resources which will speak meaningfully to the shame-based person. You are encouraged to articulate those and appropriate them accordingly. My concern is that we engage in theological and ecclesiological reclamation of these resources, not as some kind of exercise in religious fetishism or as a return to a kind of pristine pietism, but so that the historic teachings, symbols, and rituals of the faith tradition which have supported, sustained, guided, and healed the people of God in the past might also have their healing power unleashed in the present. In my opinion, this requires careful exegesis, historical analysis, theological reflection, critical hermeneutics, and informed pastoral care. It is to this final consideration of implementing the faith resources in the practice of ministry that our attention is now directed.

NOTES

1. Tillich, Paul. *The Courage to Be*. New Haven: Yale University Press, 1952, pp. 40-63.

2. Klopfenstein, Rudolf. *Scham und Schande Nach dem Alten Testament.* Zurich: Theologischer Verlag, 1972.

3. Nathanson, Donald L. (eds.) *The Many Faces of Shame.* New York: Guilford Press, 1987, p. 158.

4. Nathanson, p. 42.

5. Kaufman,Gershen. *Shame: The Power of Caring.* Cambridge: Schenkman Publishing Co., 1980.

6. Lynd, Helen. *On Shame and the Search for Identity.* New York: Harcourt, Brace and Co., 1958.

7. Erikson, Erik. *Childhood and Society.* New York: W.W. Norton and Co., 1963 (2nd ed.), pp. 251-254.

8. Erikson, pp. 261-263.

9. Pedersen, Johannes. *Israel: Its Life and Culture,* Vol. I. London: Oxford University Press, pp. 245-259.

10. Ramsey, George W. "Is Name-Giving an Act of Domination in Genesis 2:23 and Elsewhere?" *The Catholic Biblical Quarterly,* 50 (1988) 24-35. See also J. Barr. "The Symbolism of Names in the O.T." *Bulletin of John Rylands Library* 52 (1969) 20-21.

11. Tillich, Paul. *Systematic Theology* Vol. III. Chicago: University of Chicago Press, 1963, pp. 223-228.

12. Kaufman, p. 137ff.

13. Aulen, Gustaf. *Christus Victor.* New York: The Macmillan Co., 1961.

14. Wurmser, Leon. *The Mask of Shame.* Baltimore: Johns Hopkins University Press, 1981, p. 82.

15. Kaufman, p. 38.

Chapter Six

Dismantling the Shame and Embracing Freedom

It has been stressed throughout this book that a cognitive understanding of the shame issue is not sufficient to release the person from her or his shame-based orientation. An existential experience of release is imperative, so that the person not only understands intellectually the nature of the situation, but also affectively appropriates the available resources in dealing with shame.

Gershen Kaufman has outlined in detail the methodology which he employs in dealing with shame-based persons. The central focus of his approach is the necessity of restoring the interpersonal bridge.[1] He proposes a very helpful paradigm for the process of dismantling the shame, but it is devoid of the spiritual dimension.

Fossum and Mason suggest a process they call moving from shame to respect. They carefully delineate a three-phased approach to aiding their clients in making progress in dealing with their disgrace shame issues.[2] Ronald and Patricia Potter-Efron provide a variety of insights, exercises, and suggestions as they work with their clients.[3] James M. Harper and Margaret H. Hoopes approach the issue from a family-systems perspective. After an elaborate analysis dealing with the etiology of shame within a family system and assessing the various response patterns, the clinical application of their insights is suggested in the final section of their book.[4] Finally, Donald Nathanson, in his provocative work, does a masterful job of explicating the shame-pride axis, with particular emphasis upon the implications for the human experiences of sex and love.[5] These sources and many others were of immeasurable value in understanding the psychosocial dynamics of disgrace shame. The clinical insights and procedures were insightful and informed much of my own thinking on the subject. Still, references to either the theological or spiritual dimensions of shame were limited or only implied. Lewis B. Smedes' book picks up very nicely on the issues of shame and grace, but confines the scope of the discussion to that singular theological tenet.[6] It seems to me that a wider sweep of theological and spiritual considerations, particularly for those who are members of the faith community, are critically important and need to be factored into the resolution process.

It has also become evident to me over the years as a pastor that I not only need to be aware of my own shame issues, but that I need to process some of them before I can be of assistance to someone else. Obviously there will never be complete resolution of these issues given the reality of human limitations. But the danger always exists that the shame might be increased in another person as well as within myself if I have not tended to my own shame issues. From the therapeutic perspective, Andrew Morrison states,

> Each therapist must make a practice of facing and learning about his or her own shame experiences, his or her own lack of self-acceptance. Such awareness will inevitably foster attention to, and useful therapeutic work with patient's shame, which constitutes one major treatment goal of every therapeutic encounter.[7]

Morrison states that acceptance is key to the working through of these paralyzing and debilitating situations. He astutely notes that the counselor and the counselee are working mutually in this process when he writes,

> The discovery, examination, and working through of these painful feelings, and the ultimate realization that therapist and patient alike can accept them, constitute a major curative element in successful treatment. In achieving this goal, the therapist must be willing to face and acknowledge his or her own shame–his or her own failure to realize ambitions and ideals, his or her own grandiosity and defects. The therapist's avoidance of these feelings constitutes a major impediment to the treatment of shame, and explains in part the low profile of shame in the history of psychoanalytic writings.[8]

James Harper and Margaret Hoopes devote an entire chapter in their book to encouraging therapists to look at the origin, development, and nature of their own shame.[9] The same concern is applicable to anyone in the faith community who is working with the issue of shame.

The faith tradition has been instructive for me as a pastoral teacher in developing a methodology for counseling with the shame-based person or working with a group of shamed individuals. This is not to suggest that it is only someone who embraces a religious faith who can work successfully with shame-based people. Rather, it points to the fact that there is a faith context and matrix out of which the faith-oriented person operates in addressing the issue of shame. Over the past decade I have had ample opportunity in my ministry to reflect on the specific ways in which the faith tradition might both inform and be integrated into the process of liberation for those ensnared in the intricate web of disgrace shame.

For me the method has really grown out of the employment of the gifts as well as the fruits of the Spirit which the apostle Paul delineates in Galatians 5:22, "But the fruit of the Spirit is love, joy, peace, patience, kindness, goodness, faithfulness, gentleness, self-control; against such there is no law." Theologically this points to a fundamental truth, namely, that any and all healing that occurs does so by the power, gift, and the grace of God alone! God works in a variety of ways through processes and people in counseling, consolation, and conversation to effect change and transformation. Working out of the faith perspective, one can legitimately lay claim to the gifts and fruits of the Spirit which God has so generously promised and given. These gifts and "fruits of the Spirit" have been sequentially reordered to reflect a pattern which seems to be particularly appropriate when dealing with the issue of shame. The process obviously is not rigidly ordered or limited, for the Spirit works when and where it wills. I have found this method to be appropriate in dealing with shame, as well as a variety of other pastoral situations.

PATIENCE AS PRIMARY

St. Chrysostom of antiquity claimed that patience was the queen of the virtues. In a society accustomed to instantaneous gratification and immediate results, production is preferred to process, quantity to quality, speed to sensitive and deliberate movement. Patience is not only a lost virtue, it is a fruit of the Spirit which often lays unclaimed by the faith community. In processing my own shame issues and working with others in the faith community, patience is of the essence. The lack of patience is perhaps one of the reasons why so many of us continue to battle the shame problem. Shame is something which most of us would rather avoid. We deny its existence, we minimize its impact, and we rationalize the results of its working in our own lives. When we are inevitably confronted with it, we are impatient and want to dispense with it as quickly as possible.

In our counseling, "Joan" quickly identified her shame issues as stemming from her family of origin as well as messages she had picked up in her church. She assumed that because she had identified the issue, her feelings of shame would dissipate immediately. The process did not go fast enough for her. She was saying things like, "I want to be done with this stuff, now!" "I'm not sure I really want to take the time to work with these issues." Her questions betrayed the same impatience, "Is this ever going to be over?" "Does it ever get any better?" "Why is this taking so long?" or "Shouldn't I be better by now?" The shamed identity is not a condition which develops suddenly, so the expectation that it should dissipate instantaneously is unreasonable. Yet I find in myself and in others the desire to move "over" it rather than "through" it. As humans we prefer pleasure to pain and dealing with shame is a painful process. If I hope to assist others in patiently processing their shame, I need to practice what I preach in my own life.

Thus the initial exercise in patience for the would-be helper comes in dealing first of all with her or his own sense of shame. A wise friend once said to me that I should not ask others to do what I myself am unwilling to do. How can I pretend to assist others in dismantling their shame and embracing freedom, if I am not also involved in the process of dismantling my own shame? It is important to factor this into the process because the nature of shame is such that through identification and parallel process, the would-be helper can become entangled and ensnarled in the shame situation of the person seeking help. The scenario can easily turn into one of the blind leading the blind, as Jesus so aptly stated it, so that both can fall into the pit (Matthew 15:14). The pitfall is the temptation to think that the one helping is above or beyond all of the issues. Such an assumption is dangerous because it fails to take seriously our own humanity. None of us is untouched or unaffected by disgrace shame. It is indigenous to the human condition and we need to acknowledge and admit that for ourselves. This is not to suggest that the helper, pastor, or priest will have resolved all of her or his own shame issues, but a conscious awareness of the personal shame issues is critical. The Socratic injunction to "Know thy self" is particularly fitting in this setting.

Second, the would-be helper must also be patient in working with the shame-based person. It is noteworthy that the biblical word for patience is variously translated as endurance, steadfastness, or perseverance. These words are varying nuances of what patience means. As one might surmise, the shamed person is often doubtful, defensive, and despairing of any possibility for assistance or relief and this is often complicated by the fact that the person may be despondent and depressed. Silvan Tomkins points to the fact that ". . . shame, if magnified in frequency, duration and intensity such that the head is in a permanent posture of depression, can become malignant in the extreme."[10] Morrison points to the same phenomenon and notes that Kohut and Bibring implicitly agree to the fact that there is a close relationship between shame and depression and that clinical depression can ensue from a prolonged and exaggerated sense of shame.[11]

The temptation for the helper to give up is just as real as for the person who is battling the shame. Patience is that "fruit of the Spirit" for which every would-be healer must pray as she/he works with shame-based persons. Attempts to sabotage the counseling by foiling any and all approaches should be expected. It takes an immense amount of patience to refrain from scolding, accusing, or indicting the person for her or his unwillingness to cooperate. In those moments the spiritual fruits of kindness, goodness, and self-control must supplant the desire to "throw in the towel" and declare the case closed. Often the helper's own need to fix the situation or rescue the person issues in this kind of frustration. We are impatient with the person as well as ourselves as helpers and fail to trust the process in which the Spirit is leading. For the helper, repentance is often the most appropriate response to such impatience.

"Paul" and I developed a close relationship as he shared with me his struggle with shame issues throughout his life. He was intellectually intrigued by the phenomenon of disgrace shame, but could not appropriate it emotionally so as to experience a change and transformation in his own life. I felt like we were going over the same ground and the same issues, session after session. I must confess that I was becoming internally irritable and agitated with him. I interpreted his resistance to change as a deliberate attempt at frustrating the process so that he could ultimately say, "See, I told you so. This sounds good, but it doesn't work for me." After honestly sharing with him my frustration, he stated that he was not attempting to frustrate the process through resistance, but that he did not really trust that the process could help. For so many years he had struggled with his shame issues and despaired of ever being free from its clutches. He was reluctant to risk trusting the process or trusting me for fear that he would only experience yet another painful failure.

Patience, patience, patience, and more patience is needed. Paul enjoins the faith community at Thessalonica, that when dealing with the idlers, fainthearted, and weak to ". . . be patient with them all" (I Thessalonians 5:14b). I would certainly add to that list, among other situations of the human condition, the shame-based person. Patience is of the essence. The word must be indelibly inscribed in the heart of every would-be helper both for her or himself as well as the one seeking help.

FAITH AS FOUNDATIONAL

Fundamental and foundational for comprehending the process of gaining freedom from the paralyzing effects of shame is to understand the nature of faith. Faith in God, faith in others, faith in oneself, and faith in the power of the process by which "faithful" relationships are created are the key concerns of this section. Faith itself is a gift which God desires to give to all people. For me faith is not intellectual assent to a given set of dogmatic propositions, but rather it is an unqualified trust in a gracious, merciful, and loving

God who suffers with people in the midst of their pain. Faith constantly seeks understanding and that is the role played by theology. Faith may express itself intellectually in theological assertions, but faith and theology are not identical. Making this distinction is often very important for shame-based people, who may feel that they always have to have it "right."

Faith in God

Faith in God has always been foundational in the Judeo-Christian tradition. Abram trusted that the promise of Yahweh for a child would be fulfilled, even when that seemed impossible. "And he (Abram) believed (trusted) the Lord; and he (the Lord) reckoned it to him as righteousness" (Genesis 15:6). Faith in God is what accomplished deliverance at the time of the Exodus. Faith in the promise of God eventuated in entering into the promised land. The importance of faith is noted throughout the Scriptures as the conviction that God will keep God's promises irrespective of the circumstances. The writer of Hebrews says that ". . . faith is the assurance of things hoped for, the conviction of things not seen" (Hebrews 11:1). Throughout the remainder of that eleventh chapter of Hebrews, the author goes on to illustrate what is meant by faith as evidenced in the lives of God's people.

Faith in God means that God is bound by God's own faithfulness to the promises that have been made. The writer of Psalm 89 begins the hymn of praise with these words, "I will sing of thy steadfast love, O Lord, for ever; with my mouth I will proclaim thy faithfulness to all generations. For thy steadfast love was established for ever, thy faithfulness is firm as the heavens" (Psalm 89:1-2).

For many shame-based people who are a part of the community of faith, there is often considerable doubt as to whether or not God is really concerned about them or interested in their plight. In my opinion, this attitude stems not so much from their pride in having sinned so greatly that they are beyond the scope of God's grace and love, but rather from a fundamental self-perception of unworthiness, unacceptability, and unlovability. It is an image of the self that has been developed through years and years of shaming and the good news of God's faithfulness to them is incomprehensible. Attempting through rhetoric to persuade them otherwise serves only to increase the sense of shame. For some people, the transformative moment may be a sudden insight, a sudden awareness of the presence of God; but for most, the conviction that God is faithful and that faith in God is the foundation upon which life is to be built occurs as faith in others begins to develop.

Faith in Others

Shamed people have often been battered, bruised, and burned by other people who have not kept faith with them. In their relationships with others they have experienced betrayal, ridicule, violation, rejection, derision, and mockery. These experiences have left deep scars. The ability to trust and thereby have faith in others is minimal at best. Coming to believe that another can truly be faithful in a relationship requires an immense amount of time. Suspicion and fear lurk as ever-present specters for the shame-based person. How do I know that I can really trust this person? Actions do speak louder than words. The person who would help facilitate healing must prove her or himself to be faithful in the relationship.

Paramount in this whole consideration is the critical issue of confidentiality. It takes an immense amount of courage to begin to face all of the disgrace shame in one's life. I find it important to continually remind people who are processing their shame issues with me that our conversations are confidential. Disgrace shame has to do with the threat and the fear of exposure. As already noted, the impact of the shame experience is often centered in betrayal, deception, and inappropriate disclosure. Faith in the other implies faithfulness to the covenant of confidentiality.

Faith in Oneself

This may constitute the crux of the matter. By faith in oneself I do not mean that the person can extricate her or himself through exercising personal willpower or by following some self-help schema. For me, faith in oneself means believing that because I am a created child of God, I have intrinsic worth and value. I need to develop the conviction that as a person I need not apologize for my existence! Faith in oneself as a person is predicated on creation anthropology as outlined in the previous chapter. I suspect that much of the problem with regard to the self stems from the fact that the word is used in so many ways.

In traditional theology, the emphasis has often been upon denying the self. In this context, the self is symbolic of all within me that is antithetical to the way and will of God. It is that part of me that is selfish and which has no regard for others. It is epitomized in the phrase, "After me, you come first!" Selfishness, narcissism, and egocentrism characterize the "Big Ego" or the "Big Self" as it is spoken of in Alcoholics Anonymous. Certainly the slaying and death of the self, or the "old Adam" to use a biblical metaphor, is necessary before "new life" or a "transformed life" can come into existence. The reality of the selfish or the sinful self does not cancel out the truth that every person is created in the image of God. As a created self or person we are of intrinsic value and worth. It is faith in this understanding of the self that is so crucial for a shame-based person to appropriate.

Faith in the Process

Faith in God, others, and self is at best a tiny flickering flame which needs to be fanned with the life-giving wind or breath of the Spirit. As it is foundational in any relationship, trust is the sine qua non. This is especially true in dealing with a shamed person. The venture of faith or trust is the establishment, be it ever so tenuous, of the interpersonal bridge of connectedness between the shamed person and the one providing pastoral ministry. Kaufman also sees this as the initial task of any helper.[12] The inability to trust may be indicative of developmental deficiencies. Erik Erikson speaks of "trust vs. mistrust" as the first and therefore fundamental stage in his epigenetic schema of human development.[13] If some semblance of trust in one's environment and some degree of faithfulness in relationships cannot be established, it will impair all of the other developmental processes as well. It is difficult to conceive of being able to trust in God when there has been no experience of trust with another human being. While faith in God is a gift which is imparted to human beings, its appropriation experientially is predicated on some experience of trust in human relationships.

The faith perspective in dealing with shame adds an important ingredient to the mix, namely, the awareness, confidence, and faith that God is purposefully involved in this endeavor whether or not one can believe or feel that at the time. The conviction on the part of those who from a faith point of view facilitate healing claim that whatever change and healing may occur is not credited to human effort, but is singularly due to the blessing and transforming power of the Divine Spirit. As laudable and even as effective as human endeavor might be, members of the faith community are convinced that God is interested and actively involved in the emancipation of persons and groups from the debilitating power of disgrace shame.

As has already been suggested, it takes an immense amount of time, patience, perseverance, and empathetic understanding to embark upon a journey or to accompany this person on a path which must be understood as trustworthy and not treacherous. Most who are willing to take the "leap of faith" will do so only if they believe that their guide will be found faithful and will not desert or abandon them. As was noted earlier in this book, desertion or fear of abandonment is one of the dynamics of shame. A deep and manifest trust in the Spirit to guide and direct the process is essential. Integral to the establishment of this trusting relationship is the ability to be mutually disclosive. In other words, faith as trust is something which must be modeled; it does not arise out of a vacuum. Trust begets trust. Fear of relational rejection or subjection to more shaming erects a formidable barrier to healing, whether in a one-to-one relationship or a group setting.

I have found in my own counseling that the most effective way of overcoming that barrier is to share and reveal something of my own experience of shame. This approach may run counter to other forms of counseling in which personal disclosure may not be judicious, but with the shame-based person it provides an important connecting link with the struggling person. Self-disclosure not only provides a point of identification, it grants permission for that person to reveal something of her or himself. The person trusts that the situation is safe, that is, free from the threat of experiencing put-downs, derision, mockery, judgment, rejection, being laughed at, humiliation, or loss of face.

Critical in the process of mutual self-disclosure is the matter of timing and balance. By timing I mean waiting for the chairotic or optimal moment in which appropriate self-disclosure on the part of the counselor is most poignant. I don't believe that this is something which can be taught. It requires an intuitive sense of appropriateness which is a gift which must be cultivated. If the counselor reveals too much about her or himself, it may frighten the counselee or the whole group with whom she/he is working. Revealing too much too soon violates the boundaries of propriety and perhaps privacy, and can carry one into the realm of discretionary shame. The opposite extreme of revealing nothing gives cause to suspect that the helper or group facilitator is frightened, threatened, or distrustful. The key is to find the balance. This obviously varies depending upon the individual or group with whom one is working. From the faith perspective it is a matter of trusting the Spirit of God to provide the wisdom when it comes to timing and balance. To err in timing or balance is evidence of one's own humanity. Thus, persons involved in facilitating the healing process need to humbly acknowledge their own limitations. Acknowledging the same in the midst of the counseling process models faith or trust in the process itself.

The establishment of trust takes time and effort. Patient persistence rather than pushing or probing into the private realm of personal experience is required. The time needed to establish this kind of relationship varies with the person or group with whom one is working. I have had instances in which it took several months for the trust or faith relationship to develop. The counselor must also have faith in the process and believe that, in due time, healing will begin to occur. Healing is a shared experience, for as the counselor facilitates the process of dismantling the shame in the life of another human being, the counselor is simultaneously dismantling more of her or his own shame.

Throughout this section, reference has been made to the shame-based person and her or his relationship with a helper. It is important to define who the counselor might be in these situations. It certainly can be a professional relationship with a clergyperson, counselor, or someone else who is professionally credentialed to work with people who struggle with disgrace shame and other problems. In many instances, the issues are so complex that a professional referral is required. I have also discovered in my own life, that many of these debilitating experiences of shame can be effectively dealt with by honestly sharing with a fellow traveler who journeys on the path of faith. Any faithful relationship characterized by mutual trust, disclosure, confidentiality, and acceptance can be the occasion for God's Spirit to effect healing and freedom.

No one knows where the process will ultimately lead, but that too is the nature of faith. It leads us into uncharted waters or onto an untrodden path the end of which we do not know, but we trust and have faith that the Spirit of God will guide and direct us to healing and health. If faith as trust in God, others, and self forms the foundation for the healing relationship, hope must provide the lure into the future for the shame-based person. More often than not the person feels both helpless and hopeless in the face of the overwhelming power which the shame exerts.

HOPE AS CONSTITUTIVE

Even though hope is not one of the fruits of the Spirit delineated in Paul's catalog of gifts cited in Galatians 5:22, it takes its place as a gift of the spirit along with faith and love to form the dynamic triad in I Corinthians 13. Whether intentionally or inadvertently omitted from the Galatians pericope, I find it one of the essential ingredients and components for counseling with shamed persons.

A sense of hopelessness may in and of itself preclude the person's seeking out help. As a matter of fact, many people suffer the shame of shame itself! Shame is more than a vicious cycle, it is a descending spiral which intensifies with each revolution of descent. If the person seeks help, it is important to recognize and affirm this as an "act of hope" in and of itself. Many shamed people withdraw further into themselves or despair completely, which may lead them to self-abuse or self-destruction. I can remember one person who recited a litany of shameful woes and concluded with the conviction that indeed all was lost. My response was simply, "You are here." Had all hope been relinquished, the person likely would not have made even this last-ditch attempt at dealing with life.

Hope may be faint and dim, the person may be fragile and weakened; so as with faith, any flicker of the flame of hope needs to be fanned. I am reminded of the gracious demeanor of the servant described in the first servant song of Isaiah, ". . . a bruised reed he will not break, and a dimly burning wick he will not quench" (Isaiah 42:3). This has been a guiding image for my pastoral role in dealing with shame-based people. There comes a time for constructive or caring confrontation in the counseling process, but launching into that prematurely can crush what little hope may currently be present.

Hope is a lure into a more promising future that is also engendered in telling the story from the past. In order for the person to gain the maximum benefit of sharing her or his story, it is important that the individual self-consciously relate it to the issue of disgrace shame. Even as giving a name is critical to the issue of identity (see previous chapter 5), so also naming disgrace shame is important. As noted previously, many people find it difficult to give shame a name. It is a kind of general malaise, an awareness that something is not right. Sometimes it manifests itself in mild depression or inexplicable anger. Naming the experiences and feelings as shame enables the person to begin the emancipation process. In order to be free, one needs to know what it is that one is being emancipated from in life. As the trusting relationship progresses, the person is invited to share her or his story as a way of identifying the origins of the shame.

Shame sources are shared through story. In the identification and articulation of the shame, the person begins to experience some release from the past, which provides a new source of hope. It needs to be clearly stated that hope comes only through the pain of dealing constructively with the past. The natural tendency on the part of most people is to protect not only themselves, but others from the sources of shame. Loyalty to the family of origin may be the greatest single factor hindering the dismantling process. For example, the shame of defilement or feeling dirty which results from an incestuous family situation is an extremely painful reality. Protection of and loyalty to the family of origin make it difficult to identify this source of shame, yet, if there is to be any hope of being emancipated from the debilitating effects of shame, that reality needs to be confronted. Hope comes at a great price, namely breaking the conspiracy of silence surrounding the family secret.

Evidence that one is drawing close to the sources of shame is manifested in the signals and body language of the person or persons with whom one is working. The eyes, which sometimes have been called the windows to the soul, avoid contact. A physiological reaction takes places which often ushers in blushing. Instinctively, there is the "hiding of the face." The face symbolizes the being of the person to the outside world. Shame creates the risk of losing face or one's sense of integrity in relationship to others. The whole body is affected, and people often slither downward if they are in a sitting position or walk with stooped shoulders. It has been my experience, personally as well as with others, that there is a blocking of speech when shame suddenly shoots into consciousness. It is as though the vocal cords themselves were paralyzed by the debilitating effects of the shame. Some people have described the experience as a "shame attack." It strikes quickly and often unexpectedly, like a snake, and its venom soon paralyzes the entire body. Other people have described the experience as being more subtle, like the tightening coils of a python or the tentacles of an octopus. The person does not realize that she/he is in the snare or grasp until it is too late and the breath and life are slowly but systematically squeezed from the body.

All of these reactions serve to squelch the fragile feelings of hope and threaten to drive the person deeper into the shame. It is important that not only the words, but also the feelings and reactions, be processed in an accepting manner so that the person does not regress into the depths of shame.

Hope is also engendered if one can satisfactorily resolve what Kaufman calls the "shame binds."[14] These are situations in which the person feels shamed no matter what action may be taken. An example might be of a young boy who wishes to please his father by playing football, but fears being injured. If he plays and does not do well because of his fear of injury, he will likely be shamed by the coaching staff as well as his fellow competitors. He will feel shame for himself, but also shame because he has disappointed his father. On the other hand, if he refuses to participate, he will be shamed for being a "coward" or a "chicken" and will feel like he has failed his father. He feels there is no way in which he can win; he loses and suffers shame no matter what he does. Being locked into that kind of bind is not only paralyzing and debilitating, but tends to snuff out any sense of hope.

Innumerable scenarios can be imagined wherein the person feels caught in a bind with shame as the payoff no matter what the person does. It is critical that these binds be addressed and emptied of their paralyzing power or hope will wane.

It is evident that when we speak of hope, it is more than just wishful thinking or desiring that the debilitating effects of shame will vanish. Hope is born out of the conviction that God can liberate people through honest confrontation with the shame issues. This requires hard work done in faith so that hope may arise anew. One of the frustrating things I have found in dealing with shame-based people is how quickly and easily hope waxes and wanes, sometimes even within the same counseling period. Hope in the possibility of a new future which, while not devoid of shame, is not shackled by it, is very fragile. Progress toward that end is easily dashed as some shame-inducing thought, feeling, or action is recalled or introduced into the counseling situation.

As the individual or group begins to make the connection between their shame and the defenses which they have employed, a new sense of hope emerges. Cognitive understanding of the situation is only the first step in the process. The person may make the connection, for example, between her or his perfectionism as a defense and the shame dynamic of feeling deficient. Inevitably, more is required than simply making the intellectual connection. Resolution is needed so that the hope for freedom from the vicious cycle can be realized. This often involves intentional changes in behavior. Shame tends to substantiate itself through reinforcing behavior in all aspects of the person's life. Thus the *Weltanschauung* (orientation and view of life as a whole) as well as the life-style and behavior require reorientation.

LOVE AT THE CORE

"So faith, hope, love abide, these three; but the greatest of these is love." So says St. Paul in I Corinthians 13:13. In dealing with the shame-based person or group, all three dispositions are essential! However, it is love which is at the core of dismantling the shame structures in the lives of people. As we wrestle with shame in ourselves and in others, we are, according to Leon Wurmser, dealing with the issue of feeling "unloved." He says, "Basic shame is the pain of essential unlovability."[15] It may be a matter of semantics, but I have found that unlovability is synonymous with unacceptability when dealing with the issue of shame.

Theologically, the faith community has always asserted the centrality of God's love for the world. Love is the divine motivation for the unilateral establishment of the covenant with God's people. It was love which prompted God into radical and drastic action on behalf of the world (John 3:16, Ephesians 2:4-7). Restoration of the relationship between God and the creatures God has created is based on love (I John 3:1, 4:9-10). The injunction to love is as old as the faith tradition itself. (Note Deuteronomy 6:5, Leviticus 19:18 as quoted by Jesus in Matthew 22:37-40, and parallel passages.) It is God's love which makes the world go round and which is to be the determinative motivation in the relationship which people of faith have with one another (I John 4:19). The Scripture is replete with injunctions and admonitions to love one another (John 13:34, 15:12, 17, Romans 13:9, Gal. 5:14, James 2:8, I Peter 1:22, I John 3:11, 18, 23, I John 4:11-12). It is in of this context that the relationship with the shamed person is established. The distinctive thing about love which is motivated and engendered by God's love is that it is not selective, nor is it qualified or quantified by human standards. It is an unconditional love that accepts the person for what she/he is rather than what she/he might be.

God's love which was incarnate in the person of Christ is incarnated in the person of the one helping the shamed individual or group to become liberated from the debilitating effects of disgrace shame. This is accomplished in a number of different ways. Initially it is a matter of being present for and attendant to the story of the shamed person or persons. The shamed person requires the undivided attention of the listener who, as Theodor Reik once said, needs to listen with the "third ear."[16] This kind of patient presence with the person or persons strengthens the sense of trust and often provides a new experience for the shamed person. Retreat into silence or the superficial masking of feelings has been the modus operandi for so long that being given permission not only to speak the mind, but share from the heart in an environment of acceptance and love, is in and of itself a salutary experience. Quiet but intentional and attentive presence is another piece in the mosaic of effective ministry with shame-based people.

The interpersonal bridge fashioned in love is built by a concrete connectedness with the person. This is most effectively accomplished through the power of touch. In a sanitized and sterilized society, estrangement and alienation are experienced through the covert and overt distancing mechanisms which are employed to preclude significant encounters and connections with others. The healing power of touch has itself suffered from lack of use. Love is communicated through the connective action of physical touch which can effect healing. Touch conveys the grace of God's acceptance and acceptance by another human being. The Synoptics are replete with examples of Jesus touching others or their desiring to be touched by him as a means for healing. (Note Matthew 8:3, 8:15, 9:20, 9:29, 14:36, 20:34, Mark 1:41, 3:10, 5:27-31, 6:56, 7:33, 8:22, Luke 5:13, 6:19, 8:44-47, 22:51.) Even though in most instances in the Synoptics, as with the passage in James 5:13-15, the reference is to a physical illness or malady, healing does occur through touch and encompasses the whole person; body, mind and spirit. The healing power of touch is, however, not without its own unique problems.

Touch can create a powerful conflict within some shame-based persons, particularly those persons who have experienced only inappropriate touch and violating contact with other people. The healing power of touch is then obviated by the terrifying memories of what such close encounters and personal experiences have meant in the past. Add to this deep inner conflict the reality of the sexual dimensions of touch and the fact that touch can also be construed as an exercise of power and control over another person, and it creates a perplexing quandary for all involved. Touch may be required to establish connectedness and healing, but touch can also symbolize and/or call to mind powerful shaming experiences. What the person or persons most desperately need in establishing a feeling of connection through touch can also occasion revulsion and trigger an automatic repelling response.

The power of touch was graphically demonstrated in the story of "Jenny" cited in the last chapter. The breakthrough with Jenny occurred one day after several months of counseling. She finally developed a sufficient amount of trust in the relationship with me to share her source of shame. It was an emotionally and physically convulsive experience. When the shame was verbalized she physically got up from her chair and ran to a corner of my office and began to sob uncontrollably. After some time, I gently took her by the arm and seated myself in a chair close to her and for a period of time just held her hand. Initially she was resistive to the touch and the connectedness, but she soon eased her posture. In some moments of prayerful reflection, the shame issues were processed and she left. At the beginning of our next session together she said, "Your holding my hand the last time we were together was the first experience of God's grace I've had in years. I felt loved and accepted as I was with all of my shame." This was not the end of the struggle for Jenny, but it was a significant breakthrough as the shame in her life which had held her in bondage for so many years was starting to be dismantled.

Jenny's initial response to my gentle touch was one of resistance and perhaps even suspicion. Given the issues involved with human sexuality, particularly with those people who have been sexually abused, the utilization of touch needs to be done with great care and consideration.

One solution to this conundrum is to ritualize the touch through a liturgical process which separates, and therefore objectifies, the relationship and frees it from focusing on the pain of the past and the sexual overtones of the present. It has been my personal as well as professional experience that love as healing acceptance occurs in the liturgical service of healing wherein the touch is ritualized through the laying on of hands and anointing the person with oil. The utilization of oil for anointing is not a charlatan ploy of magical hocus-pocus or an appeal to liturgical histrionics, but rather it is a reclaimed resource of the faith tradition enjoined by Scripture (James 5:14). The ritual has been utilized throughout the history of the church as a symbol of Divine love, acceptance, and healing. Love needs to be concretized for the shame-based person, rather than remaining an abstraction. The ritual for healing has proven to be a type of sacramental experience which provides an effective incarnational ministry for shame-based people. This kind of ritual not only provides a tactile avenue of connectedness, but also ensures an environment of safety and security, since the service is a public experience of worship. The ministry of touch perhaps too emotionally volatile in the privacy of the counselor or clergyperson's office, becomes a means of communicating love and healing in a public ritual. It emphasizes the importance of community itself as a healing agent. In order to accomplish this purpose, for those people or communities who are not familiar with this liturgical rite, education and explanation are obviously in order.

Love is at the core for all those desiring to work with shame-based people and is the sine qua non for facilitating release from disgrace shame. Within the faith tradition, it is expressed in an incarnational theology which embraces the reality of God's presence being mediated through Word, Sacrament, and the faith community itself with all of its rites and rituals. Love must be demonstrated, modeled, and incarnated if it is to have an impact. Love can break down the dividing walls of defenses which separate and isolate people from one another, while at the same time fostering the spirit of acceptance, integrity, worth, and value for the shame-based person.

COMMUNITY AS HEALING AGENT

In a society which emphasizes individualism, self-help, self-determination and where a "pull yourself up by your own bootstraps" philosophy prevails, shame takes a greater toll because one feels shamed for having to reach out. The acute pain of the shame-based person is exacerbated by the fact that asking for or seeking help is one more plank in the shame platform upon which the person stands. For some people it is pride which precludes asking for help. For many it is a shame issue. Asking for assistance may be construed as being a form of weakness and a diminishment of one's integrity, honor, or good name. It has been my observation that fear is a far more dominant dynamic for the shame-based person than pride. There is the fear of self-disclosure occasioned by the fear of getting hurt, exploited, or used. There is the fear of possible betrayal, abandonment, or rejection which results in the fear of experiencing greater hurt and humiliating shame. Though painfully lonely and even shame-inducing, the safety and security of isolation is often preferred to the risk of reaching out or even allowing someone else to reach out. It is evident how shame results not only in a vicious cycle, but a downwardly spiraling experience.

Community as healing agent is a critical component in the process of recovering from disgrace shame. As has been suggested, the "community" initially may be only the counselor and the shame-based person. When, through patience, faith as trust is established, hope engendered, and love demonstrated, the individual may be ready for the next significant step, which is to connect with other shame-based people who are in the recovery process. Once again timing and balance are important. An intuitive sense of readiness is required in consultation with the person who is suffering from the shame. When the person seems ready to give consideration to this step, it can be suggested not only as a possibility, but also as an indication of the healing and growth which has already occurred. It is not prudent to force the person into a group setting, but it should be suggested as another step forward in the process of recovery.

An example may be dealing with people in the faith community who have suffered the pain of divorce. Even though divorce is becoming an action which has less stigma or shame attached to it in society as a whole, I have found that with the faith community it is often fraught with the shame of failure. After counseling with a number of individuals who were experiencing the pain, grief, and shame of divorce, it was suggested that perhaps they begin to meet as a group in order to process their issues. Once the leap of faith was made to do that, the participants discovered that not only relief, but also healing, was the result of their candid and open sharing. This eventuated in a support group which grew in numbers and strength as these people became bonded together around a common concern. Having faced the shame they were experiencing, it became possible for them to face the faith community and to participate in worship and other activities. They discovered that some of their concern was a projection of their own fears onto the larger body. Even in those situations where moralistic and judgmental attitudes were encountered, the strength derived from the support group made it possible to endure and survive such experiences. The individual participants and the group as a whole began to gain further support and strength from the larger community of faith and to appropriate the benefits and gifts derived from their corporate identity.

The Spirit's gift of community may be among the most under-utilized of all. This is due in part to the individualistic emphasis in our society as a whole, as noted previously, but it may also be due to the fact that true community is infrequently experienced in our contemporary religious institutions. Community is not something which can be fabricated or created by gimmicks. It needs to be appropriated as a gift that is given by the Spirit. For the primitive Christian community, as noted in the last chapter, the essence of its experience and expression is found in Acts 2:42, where it states that the early disciples, ". . . devoted themselves to the apostles' teaching and fellowship, to the breaking of bread and prayers." The community was bonded together by common rituals, practices, and experiences which strengthened them individually and corporately. This became increasingly important when persecution was experienced. Identity, strength, nurture, purpose, and direction were derived from the Spirit-led community. The exigencies of life were not only endured, but appropriated in such a way so as to strengthen the individual and the whole community (Romans 5:3-5). It might be said that the gift of community, in whatever form it assumed, was the key to survival and even growth of the early faith community. Through study, fellowship, prayer, and sacramental participation in the rites and rituals, it was possible to face life with all of its vicissitudes.

This is not to suggest that the faith community was group therapy as it is known today, but it was a therapeutic community, for it was as the Greek verb *therapeuo* suggests, a "healing" community. The Scriptural tradition is rich and replete with references wherein the community experiences the healing power of God, whether through direct divine agency or the utilization of human agency. My suggestion is that at least one of the major purposes for the community of faith is to be a healing agent in the world. The healing of shame is an important part of the community's mission, since so many people are crippled and incapacitated by the power of shame. Acknowledging and naming the shame while coming face to face with its power and pervasiveness enables the members of the faith community to face one another. Through the healing gifts provided by God for the community, new hope and new life become possibile under the aegis of God's Spirit. This is not to say that shame can be easily shed by following a few simple suggestions, because it is endemic to the human condition. Rather it is an invitation for the faith community to utilize the gifts and the fruits of the Spirit in order to be liberated from the debilitating effects of shame.

A contemporary example of such processing occurs in the group experience of Alcoholics Anonymous, as well as in its spin-off companion groups. Key to the dismantling of the shame which accompanies an addiction is the capacity to articulate not only the guilt, but the shame, and to name it within the context of a loving and accepting community. The AA meeting provides such an occasion and atmosphere. There is not only the verbalization of the "wrong" which was done, which implies the guilt incurred for detrimental and damaging behavior, but the person is given permission to speak about the nature of the wrong and all of its attendant implications. This is where the shame is dealt with, whether it is identified as such or not. The person has the opportunity to acknowledge and admit not only that she/he is an alcoholic with alcoholic behavior, but to say that "I" am an alcoholic, which gets to the shame issue. The guilt deals with the behavior which has hurt and harmed so many people, including the alcoholic. Confession, absolution, forgiveness, and reconciliation are in order and are accomplished through the working of the twelve steps. The added dimension involves speaking to the issue of ontology, that is, my own sense of being, value, and worth as a person. The overt and covert message of the group is, "You are accepted." Judgmentalism is precluded because there is no hierarchical evaluation of people's behavior or worth. The group has learned that accepting people for who they are is a key to recovery. In my judgment, this means that they have spoken directly to the issue of shame. The faith community can utilize this same process whereby people can deal more effectively with their shame issues.

Members of the community who desire healing from their shame have an opportunity to be engaged in that healing process. It may be a prayer group in which the participants offer up to God their struggles with their shame and ask for strength, courage, and a rich measure of the Spirit to effect change. It may be a support group in which trusting relationships have been developed and where through mutual disclosure the power of disgrace shame is diminished. Like other support groups, the opportunity is present to make and sustain contact with others in the group if an individual feels particularly vulnerable to the shame between meetings. Those who covenant together to form such a group must be intentional about their purpose in gathering and pledge themselves in good faith to be a caring and a healing community.

The community is not only a healing or therapeutic community, it also champions wholeness and health for its constituency by attending to those issues which occasion the intense and debilitating dynamics of disgrace shame. Emphasizing the worth and value of every human being irrespective of race, color, creed, economic, or ethnic background is a critical task. That is to say that the community needs to take seriously its corporate responsibility every time a new member is incorporated, whether as an infant or an adult. As an antidote to the debilitating effects of shame, the community takes seriously the building up of the body of Christ as enjoined by the writer of Ephesians (4:12-15). This intentional movement toward health through the Spirit is a preventative measure which can be exercised in the faith community.

This process should begin very early in the life of community members. Infants have a sense of whether they are loved by the way in which they are handled and treated. Toddlers sense whether they are accepted or not by others. When the community is intentional in its educational program, in its worship life, and in its manner of relating to one another, it has the capacity to build up its members so that they become mature in their own self-image as a created child of God, as well as becoming more mature in relationship to others. Rather than being a source of shame and shaming, the faith community becomes a place where a healthy individual and corporate self-image can be developed. The interaction of a community when it builds up diminishes the power of disgrace shame. When an environment of building up rather than tearing down through shame prevails, healing and health are the result.

PEACE AND JOY AS GIFT

Shame is not only debilitating, it is also a disruptive factor in the stream of life. A pervasive sense of uneasiness, uncertainty, and unsettledness creates a malaise which is malignant and metastasizes not only within the individual, but also in significant others who are closely associated with the shame-based person. Dismantling the shame can be a long and involved process, as has already been noted. Establishing the trust relationship, engendering hope, experiencing love, and becoming integrated into some kind of meaningful community are processes which require patience on the part of all involved, but ultimately they eventuate in the gifts of the Spirit, which are peace and joy.

From the perspective of faith, peace does not necessarily mean absence of conflict, nor does it mean that the person will never again be exposed to shame-inducing situations or experience the pain of shame. Since shame is indigenous to the human situation, overcoming it will be a struggle which all of us will be engaged in throughout life. However, this reality does not preclude the possibility of experiencing Spirit-given peace (John 14:25-28). At the core of this peace given by the Spirit is the promise that the person will not succumb to the troubling and fearful exigencies of life. The biblical image which serves to illustrate this point is the episode of Jesus and his disciples on the sea (Mark 4:35-41 and parallels). As long as Peter kept his eyes fixed upon the Master, his life was not threatened. But once he turned his face away he was overcome with fear and began to sink. Those who process their shame from the faith perspective learn to trust and to keep their eyes fixed upon the source of their strength and stability, which gives them their sense of equanimity and equilibrium. The faith perspective does not protect people from the shame-inducing situations of everyday life, but rather it provides a way through such situations by embracing them for what they are and processing them accordingly. The fruit of such a disposition toward life is a sense of peace and serenity.

One of the faith resources which many find of value is that of prayer and meditation. Prayer is practicing the presence of God and placing oneself at God's disposal so as to allow the Spirit to work for peace within. As persons or groups begin to be grasped by the

Ground of Being[17] and allow themselves to be led by the Spirit to meditate on the center of their existence, the focus of attention shifts from the self to God, and peace results. It is a process of surrendering shame so that it might be supplanted by the peace of God. The letting-go of the shame is similar to the letting-go of the addictive process, which recognizes that release and redemption come not from within, but from without. A transformation comes over the individual, as there is a turning point from fixation on shame to focus on the healing power of God. Many people discover that the routine of prayer and meditation as a daily ritual is critical. Visibility, volume, and verbosity as Jesus already points out in Matthew 6:5-8 are not as critical as consistency, concentration, and congruence in prayer. Prayer is not a vehicle used to manipulate the Divine to achieve the desired end of peace. Rather, peace is granted to the one who openly desires the blessing and gift of Divine Presence in her or his life. The perspective on prayer changes from a kind of personal piety, wherein the human being speaks and expects God to answer, to an attitude which allows God to speak, so that the person may listen to the Word which God wishes to communicate.

The shame-based person then begins to experience that "peace which the world cannot give" (John 14:27). It is a peace which passes all human understanding. It is a peace which holds people together while their world may be crumbling in pieces around them. The shame-based person knows that one cannot eliminate or eradicate disgrace shame from the world or one's own life. It is here to stay as part of the human situation, but there are changes which can be made in that individual's life as the resources of faith are drawn upon and utilized for the purpose of healing. Carl Schneider says this with regard to the human situation and the brokenness occasioned by disgrace shame,

But if there is brokenness, there are also at least occasions of partial fulfillment and realizations of wholeness. In these moments, we transcend shame, and experience a higher shamelessness in which we enjoy our being and our acceptance. An overpowering grace allows us to move beyond the estrangement of disgrace and the need to respond with shame.[18]

It is important that the shame-based person focus on the issues where change is possible, namely, the attitudes and the actions for which she/he is responsible. Many of us spend much of our time, energy, and resources attempting to change those things over which we have no control, while ignoring those things about which we can do something.

The members of the faith community, like all others, need to accept the fact that disgrace shame will not disappear. But this does not leave a person hopeless or helpless. Rather than dealing with the shame through defense strategies spoken of in an earlier chapter, it is better to accept and embrace the shame and, by the grace and mercy of God, take responsibility for one's own healing. Trust in God results in a peace which points to the confidence which the faith community has in the God of love. A brief prayer in German which graces the wall of my study says it well:

> *Leg alles still in Gottes ewige Haende Das Glueck, den Schmerz, den Anfang und das Ende.*

> (Place everything confidently in God's eternal hands, your good fortune, your pain, your beginning, and your ending.)

God's peace is the gift which the shamed person desperately needs. This does not promise the end of struggle or preclude relapses into the shame system, but rather it engenders a confidence and certitude that despite what may happen, nothing will separate us from the love of God (Romans 8:31-38). That kind of peace is the companion of true joy.

Paul speaks of joy as another of the fruits of the Spirit. Joy is not to be confused with the popular injunction to be happy, which is a kind of superficial view of life. Rather it is a gift which is given to the faithful who realize the importance of God's claim upon their lives. If peace provides a sense of confidence, joy engenders a sense of security. Joy is basking in the knowledge that the cross is God's shame-bearing symbol for the world. It ensures and secures liberation from shouldering the shame for the self, and therefore provides a new perspective on life. For some people, making the sign of the cross can be a visual and tactile reminder of this truth. There is one who has borne both the sin and the shame of the world for all humankind. The security of being claimed and named by God points to the Sacrament of Baptism. In some communities the sign of the cross is part of the symbolization ritually integrated into the baptismal service. This reality is the true source of joy for the individual, but is also the occasion for joy within the community. Even though this baptismal sign is indelibly inscribed upon the person, for many individuals it needs to be constantly impressed upon them.

One shamed individual with whom I worked felt neither the safety nor the assurance of a relationship with God. This judgment was based upon the counselee's subjective feelings of worthlessness, disgust with the self, defilement, defectiveness, and deficiency. Rather than denying these feelings or trying to convince the person that such judgments were erroneous, I suggested that instead of focusing on the self, the person should look in the mirror each morning upon arising and each evening when retiring and simply say, "I am a child of God." I said perhaps the sign of the cross might reinforce that reality, so that the message would not come from within with its cutting condemnations, but rather would be a message of acceptance and affirmation coming from without. The shame was so strong that initially there was resistance to even doing the exercise, but the person finally found it possible to say those words and to hear them.

Joy is found within the fellowship of the faithful, for it is a gift which needs to be shared in relationships. Paul's epistles are replete with statements about the joy that he experiences in relationship to others (Romans 15:32, Philippians 2:2, I Thessalonians 2:20, etc.). This kind of joy is not artificially concocted, nor does it necessitate constant reinforcement and stimulation. Rather it rises spontaneously as a gift of the Spirit in response to the love and mercy of God. Joy is a fruit of the Spirit which is to be experienced and lived rather than talked about. The shame-based person is more convinced by living models of joy than by exhortations to exhibit joy. It is contagious when demonstrated within the faith community, and the shame-based person needs to see evidence of joy as a sign of hope for a new future. Thus, joy is not a perpetual emotional high, but the gift of hope and assurance lived out in faith. As with all gifts of the Spirit, they are but a temporal foretaste of the fullness of God's benevolent love consummated at the eschaton. For the person shackled in shame, joy as a fruit of the Spirit represents a new experience and a new perspective on life.

CONCLUSION

In ending this discussion, we circle back to Jan's story with which we began. It is a familiar story for many of us. The names, the circumstances, the dynamics, the experiences, and the relationships may be different, but the common denominator which binds us together is the painful awareness of the debilitating and paralyzing effects of disgrace shame. Unless the denial factor is very strong, most of us are compelled to admit that not only guilt, but also shame, plagues us on life's way. The critical issue is the manner in which we deal with it, face it, embrace it, and utilize its existence as an opportunity to grow and develop. Patton summarizes it well when he states, "What we suffer from in our shame is not a disease to be cured, but a dimension of the human condition to be experienced, shared, and used as a dynamic for change."[19] As has already been suggested, valuable information and insights are provided for us in the social sciences. But in order to be holistic in our approach to human beings, the faith dynamic needs to be factored into the whole scenario.

The path to recovery from disgrace shame is often a long and arduous journey fraught with frustrations, reversals, and disappointments. It is my contention that there are resources within the faith tradition available to those who belong to the community of faith which have been untapped, some of which I have suggested in this book. It must be recognized that those delineated in this book are those which I have found useful from my own understanding of the tradition and in my own work. I am not suggesting that this represents the totality of the resources which are available, nor am I contending that those articulated have been plumbed to the depths. It remains for each reader to reflect on her or his own understanding of the faith tradition and to appropriate the dynamics accordingly.

While there is commonality in the shame experience, it must always be remembered that each individual or group is unique. Shame and the experience of shame is nuanced in so many different ways that one must be cautious not to make assumptions, but rather to allow each person or group to deal with those concerns which are foremost in their consciousness.

When it comes to the issue of dismantling the shame, creativity is called for in each instance. Each person, group, or community must draw upon the resources, symbols, rituals, and activities which best suit the situation. This obviously will vary not only from person to person, but from culture to culture. It remains the task of each person who would facilitate the dismantling of shame to be cognizant of these personal and cultural variations. Themes, ideas, strategies, and counseling must be adapted accordingly. What I have suggested by way of content and methodology for dealing with shame from a faith perspective is paradigmatic at best. Each person is encouraged to develop her or his own way of personally and professionally dealing with the issue of disgrace shame from a theological and pastoral perspective.

My personal concern is to create, develop, and implement a process for dealing with disgrace shame which takes seriously the resources of the faith tradition. We need to engage in theological and ecclesiological reclamation of these resources, not as some kind of exercise in religious fetishism or as a return to some kind of pristine pietism, but so that the historic teachings, symbols, and rituals of the faith tradition which have supported, sustained, guided, and healed the people of God in the past might also have their healing power unleashed in the present and future. This involves careful exegesis, historical analysis, theological reflection, critical hermeneutics, and informed pastoral care practices.

The task of the faith community is to creatively integrate the faith tradition through word, ritual, sacrament, and action in ways appropriate to the person and her or his culture. This must be done in such a way that it is not only cognitively persuasive to the shame-based person, but, more important, in such a way that it can be affectively appropriated and experienced. The purpose is to effect liberation from the stranglehold of disgrace shame and to heal from its malignant properties.

NOTES

1. Kaufman, Gershen. *Shame: The Power of Caring.* New York: Schenkman Publishing Co., 1980, pp. 137-185.

2. Fossum, Merle and Marilyn Mason. *Facing Shame: Families in Recovery.* New York: W.W. Norton, 1986, pp. 166-186.

3. Potter-Efron, Ronald and Patricia. *Letting Go of Shame.* Center City, MN: Hazelden, 1989.

4. Harper, James and Margaret Hoopes. *Uncovering Shame.* New York: W.W. Norton, 1990, pp. 171-299.

5. Nathanson, Donald. *Shame and Pride.* New York: W. W. Norton, 1992.

6. Smedes, Lewis. *Shame and Grace.* San Francisco: Harper, 1993.

7. Morrison, Andrew P. "The Eye Turned Inward: Shame and the Self." In Donald L. Nathanson (ed.), *The Many Faces of Shame.* New York: Guilford Press, 1987, p. 290.

8. Morrison, p. 281.

9. Harper and Hoopes, pp. 171-186.

10. Tomkins, Silvan S. "Shame." In Donald L. Nathanson (ed.), *The Many Faces of Shame.* New York: Guilford Press, 1987, p. 150.

11. Morrison, p. 280.

12. Kaufman, p. 138.

13. Erikson, Erik. *Childhood and Society.* New York: W.W. Norton, 1963 (2nd ed.), pp. 247-251.

14. Kaufman, pp. 44-51.

15. Wurmser, Leon. *The Mask of Shame.* Baltimore: Johns Hopkins University Press, 1981, p. 93.

16. Reik, Theodore. *Listening with the Third Ear.* New York: Farrar, Straus and Co., 1952.

17. Tillich, Paul. *Systematic Theology, Vol I.* Chicago: University of Chicago Press, 1951, pp. 155-159.

18. Schneider, Carl D. *Shame, Exposure and Privacy.* Boston: Beacon Press, 1977, p. 139.

19. Patton, John. *Is Human Forgiveness Possible?* Nashville: Abingdon Press, 1985, p. 61.

Bibliography

Adler, A. *The Individual Psychology of Alfred Alder: A Systematic Presentation in Selections from His Writings.* Edited by H. L. and R. R. Ansbacher. New York: Harper, 1956.

Alexander, F. "Remarks about the relationship of inferiority feelings to guilt feelings." *International Journal of Psychoanalysis.* 1938, Vol. 19, pp. 41-49.

Augsburger, D. *Counseling in a Cross-Cultural Setting.* Philadelphia: Westminster Press, 1986.

Aulen, G. *Christus Victor.* New York: The Macmillan Company, 1961.

Ausubel, D. "Relationships between shame and guilt in the socializing process." *Psychological Review.* 1955, Vol. 62, pp. 378-390.

Beattie, M. *Codependent No More.* Center City, MN: Hazelden Publishing Co.

Becker, E. *The Denial of Death.* New York: Free Press, 1973.

Berne, E. *The Games People Play.* New York: Grove Press, 1964.

Black, C. *It Will Never Happen to Me.* Denver: M.A.C. Printing and Publications Division, 1981.

Boszormenyi-Nagy and G.M. Spark. *Invisible Loyalties.* New York: Harper and Row, 1973.

Bowen, M. *Family Therapy in Clinical Practice.* New York: Jason Aronson, 1978.

Bradshaw, J. *Healing the Shame that Binds You.* Deerfield Beach, FL: Health Communications Inc., 1988.

Broucek, F. "Shame and its relationship to early narcissistic development." *International Journal of Psychoanalysis.* 1982, Vol. 65, pp. 369-378.

Brown, J.C. and C.R. Bohn (eds). *Christianity, Patriarchy and Abuse.* New York: Pilgrim Press, 1989.

Bussert, J. *Battered Women.* Philadelphia: Division for Mission in North America-Lutheran Church in America, 1986.

Courtois, C. *Healing the Incest Wound: Adult Survivors in Therapy.* New York: W.W. Norton, 1988.

Erikson, E. *Identity and Youth in Crisis.* New York: W.W. Norton, 1968.

Erikson, E. *Childhood and Society.* New York: W.W. Norton and Co., 1963 (2nd ed.).

Erikson, E. *Identity and the Life Cycle,* Psychological Issues 1. New York: International Universities Press, 1959.

Fortune, M. *Sexual Violence: The Unmentionable Sin.* New York: Pilgrim Press, 1983.

Fortune, M. Lecture presented at Luther Northwestern Theological Seminary on January 26, 1990.

Fossum, M.A. and Mason, J. *Facing Shame: Families in Recovery.* New York: W.W. Norton, 1986.

Gilligan, C. *In a Different Voice.* Cambridge, MA: Harvard University Press, 1982.

Grinker, R. "Growth, inertia and shame: Their therapeutic implications and dangers." *International Journal of Psychoanalysis.* 1955, Vol. 36, pp. 242-253.

Harper, J. M. and M. H. Hoopes. *Uncovering Shame.* New York: W.W. Norton, 1990.

Horney, K. *Neurosis and Human Growth: The Struggle Towards Self-Realization.* New York: W.W. Norton and Co., 1950.

Horney, K. *Our Inner Conflicts.* New York: W.W. Norton and Co., 1945.

Horowitz, M. "Self-righteous rage and the attribution of blame." *Archives of General Psychology.* 1981, Vol. 38, pp. 133-138.

Jacobson, E. *The Self and the Object of the World.* New York: International Universities Press, 1964.

Jungel, E. *God as the Mystery of the World.* Grand Rapids: Eerdmans, 1983.

Kaufman, G. *The Psychology of Shame.* New York: Springer Publishing Company, 1989.

Kaufman, G. *Shame: The Power of Caring.* Cambridge: Schenkmen Publishing Company, 1980.

Kaufman, G. "The meaning of shame. Towards a self-affirming identity." *Journal of Counseling Psychology.* 1974, Vol. 21, pp. 568-574.

Kinston, W. "A Theological context for shame." *International Journal of Psychoanalysis*. 1982, Vol. 64, pp. 213-226.

Kittel, G. (ed). *Theological Dictionary of the New Testament,* Vol. 1. Grand Rapids: Wm. B. Eerdmans Publishing Company, 1964.

Klopfenstein, R. *Scham und Schande Nach dem Alten Testament.* Zurich: Theologischer Verlag, 1972.

Kohut, H. *The Analysis of the Self.* New York: International Universities Press, 1971.

Kurtz, E. *Shame and Guilt: Characteristics of the Dependency Cycle.* Center City, MN: Hazelden Publications, 1981.

Lansky, M. R. "Violence, shame and the family." *International Journal of Family Psychiatry.* 1984, Vol. 5, pp. 21-40.

Lansky, M. R. "On blame." *International Journal of Psychoanalytic Psychotherapy.* 1980, Vol. 8, pp. 429-456.

Levin, S. "The psychoanalysis of shame." *International Journal of Psychoanalysis.* 1971, Vol. 52, pp. 355-362.

Lewis, H. B. *Shame and Guilt in Neurosis.* New York: International Universities Press, 1971.

Lewis, H. B. "The role of shame in depression." In M. Rutter, C. Izard and P. Rad (eds.), *Depression in Young People: Development and Clinical Perspectives.* New York: Guilford Press, 1986.

Lindsay-Hartz, J. "Contrasting experiences of shame and guilt." *American Behavioral Scientist.* 1984, Vol. 27, pp. 689-704.

Lynd, H. M. *On Shame and the Search for Identity.* New York: Science Editions, 1961.

Mead, G. H. *Mind, Self and Society.* Chicago: Chicago University Press, 1934.

Miller, S. *The Shame Experience.* Hillsdale, NJ: The Analytic Press, 1985, p. 140.

Miller, W. *Why Christians Break Down.* Minneapolis: Augsburg Publishing House, 1973.

Minuchin, S. *Families and Family Therapy.* Cambridge, MA: Harvard University Press, 1974.

Morrison, A. P. "Shame, ideal self, and narcissism." *Contemporary Psychoanalysis.* 1983, Vol. 18, pp. 295-318.

Nathanson, D. L. (ed.). *The Many Faces of Shame.* New York: Guilford Press, 1987.

144 SHAME: A FAITH PERSPECTIVE

Nathanson, D. L. *Shame and Pride: Affect, Sex and the Birth of the Self.* New York: W.W. Norton, 1992.
Otto, R. *The Idea of the Holy.* New York: Oxford University Press, 1958.
Patton, John. *Is Human Forgiveness Possible?* Nashville: Abingdon Press, 1985.
Pedersen, J. *Israel: Its Life and Culture,* Vol. I. London: Oxford University Press 1926. Reprint No. 4, 1964.
Piers, G. and M. B. Singer. *Shame and Guilt: A Psychoanalytic and a Cultural Study.* New York: Norton, 1967.
Potter-Efron, Ronald and Patricia. *Letting Go of Shame.* Center City, MN: Hazelden, 1989.
Ramsey, G. W. "Is Name-Giving an Act of Domination in Genesis 2:23 and Elsewhere?" *The Catholic Biblical Quarterly.* 1988, Vol. 50. No. 1, January (1988) pp. 24-35.
Rank, O. *The Trauma of Birth.* New York: R. Brunner, 1952.
Reik, T. *Listening with the Third Ear.* New York: Farrar, Straus and Company, 1952.
Satir, V. *Cojoint Family Therapy.* Palo Alto: Science and Behavior Books, 1967.
Satir, V. *People Making.* Palo Alto: Science and Behavior Books, 1972.
Schaef, A. W. *Woman's Reality.* Minneapolis: Winston Press, 1981.
Schaef, A. W. *Co-dependence: Misunderstood-Mistreated.* San Francisco: Harper and Row, 1986.
Schneider, C. D. *Shame, Exposure and Privacy.* Boston: Beacon Press, 1977.
Smedes, L. B. *Shame and Grace.* San Fransisco: Harper and Collins, 1993.
Steinmetz, S. K. and M. Straus (eds.). *Violence in the Family.* New York: Harper and Row, 1975.
Thrane, G. "Shame and the construction of the self." *Annual of Psychoanalysis.* 1979, Vol. 7, pp. 321-341.
Tillich, P. *The Courage to Be.* New Haven: Yale University Press, 1952.
Tillich, P. *Systematic Theology,* Vol. 1. Chicago: University of Chicago Press 1951. 8th printing, 1963.
Tournier, P. *Guilt and Grace.* New York: Harper and Row, 1962.

Tournier, P. *Secrets.* Atlanta: John Knox Press, 1963.

Woititz, J. *Adult Children of Alcoholics.* Hollywood, FL: Health Communications Inc., 1983.

Wurmser, L. *The Hidden Dimension.* New York: Jason Aronson, 1978.

Wurmser, L. *The Mask of Shame.* Baltimore: Johns Hopkins University Press, 1981.

Index

Colorado Christian University
Library
180 S. Garrison
Lakewood, Colorado 80226